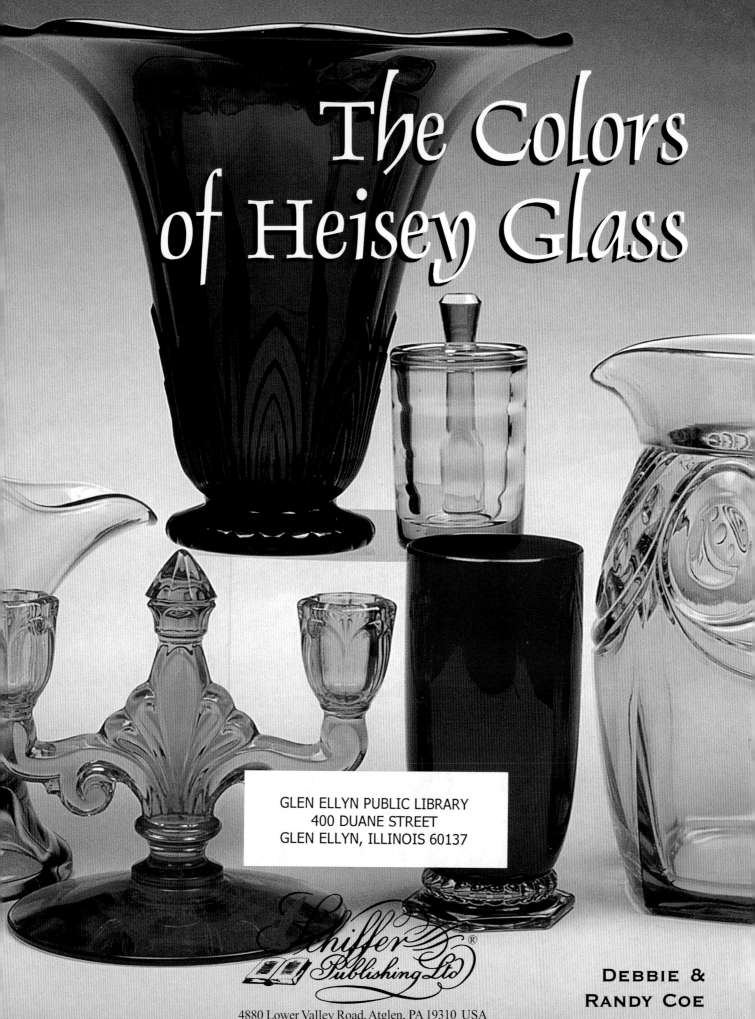

The Colors
of Heisey Glass

Schiffer Publishing Ltd

4880 Lower Valley Road, Atglen, PA 19310 USA

DEBBIE &
RANDY COE

Other Schiffer Books by Debbie and Randy Coe
Elegant Glass: Early, Depression & Beyond
Liberty Blue Dinnerware
Glass Animals & Figurines
Avon's 1876 Cape Cod Collection Glass Dinnerware
Fenton Burmese Glass
Fenton Glass Baskets Acanthus to Hummingbird
Fenton Glass Baskets Innovation to Wisteria & Numbers
Animal Pitchers

Title page photo: Top: Stiegel Blue vase, Zircon Saturn mustard
Bottom: Flamingo Bonnet basket, Blue duo candle holder,
Tangerine tumbler, Moongleam Ipswich pitcher

Library of Congress Cataloging-in-Publication Data

Coe, Debbie.
  The colors of Heisey glass / Debbie & Randy Coe.
      p. cm.
  Includes bibliographical references and index.
  ISBN 0-7643-2507-8 (hardcover)
  1. A.H. Heisey & Co.—Catalogs. 2. Heisey pressed
glass—Collectors and collecting—United States—Catalogs.
3. Glass, Colored—Collectors and collecting—United
States—Catalogs. I. Coe, Randy. II. Title.

NK5198.A23A4 2006
748.2917154—dc22
                                           2006006750

Designed by "Sue"
Type set in CopperplateGothic Bd BT/Souvenir Lt BT

ISBN: 0-7643-2507-8
Printed in China
1 2 3 4

Published by Schiffer Publishing Ltd.
4880 Lower Valley Road
Atglen, PA 19310
Phone: (610) 593-1777; Fax: (610) 593-2002
E-mail: Info@schifferbooks.com

For the largest selection of fine reference books on this and
related subjects, please visit our web site at
www.schifferbooks.com
We are always looking for people to write books on new and
related subjects. If you have an idea for a book please
contact us at the above address.

This book may be purchased from the publisher.
Include $3.95 for shipping.
Please try your bookstore first.
You may write for a free catalog.

In Europe, Schiffer books are distributed by
Bushwood Books
6 Marksbury Ave.
Kew Gardens
Surrey TW9 4JF England
Phone: 44 (0) 20 8392-8585; Fax: 44 (0) 20 8392-9876
E-mail: info@bushwoodbooks.co.uk
Website: www.bushwoodbooks.co.uk
Free postage in the U.K., Europe; air mail at cost.

CONTENTS

ACKNOWLEDGEMENTS 4

PREFACE 5

INTRODUCTION 6
    MEASUREMENTS 16
    VALUE GUIDE 16

1. THE COLORS OF HEISEY GLASS 18
    ALEXANDRITE 18
    AMBER 24
    CANARY 29
    CRYSTAL 31
    DAWN 56
    EMERALD 62
    FLAMINGO 68
    HAWTHORNE 89
    IVORINA VERDE AND IVORY 95
    MARIGOLD 100
    MOONGLEAM 105
    OPAL 128
    SAHARA 129
    STIEGEL BLUE 141
    TANGERINE 153
    ZIRCON/LIMELIGHT 157

2. EXPERIMENTAL COLORS 171

3. THE DECORATING COMPANIES 176

COLLECTORS' ORGANIZATIONS 190

BIBLIOGRAPHY 191

INDEX 192

The Original Heisey crest used on the back of the Catalog and Price List No. 31 September 1950

Acknowledgements

Without such a wonderful bunch of people contributing various aspects of information, this book could not contain the vast of amount material it does. It is because of the wonderful collectors, so willing to share their glass, that all the photographs in this book exist.

Neila and Tom Bredehoft are authors of numerous Heisey books as well as board members of the West Virginia Museum of American Glass. Neila also serves as editor of *All About Glass*, the museum's quarterly newsletter. With such valuable knowledge between them, they were a great resource for information. Many bits of their information are included in this book. They also graciously read our draft and made changes for us. We feel privileged to know them.

Darlene and Gordon Cochran were important contributors to this book. Gordon had previously served on the Board of Directors of Heisey Collectors of America for several years and shared his knowledge of Heisey. They opened their home to us and allowed us to photograph their large collection. In addition, they furnished some much-needed information about items. They were a huge benefit in reviewing our material. Their generosity gives new meaning to "dedicated collectors," so willing to share.

Jim Cooke was a supporter of this book. He allowed us to photograph his collection and provided some nice archival pieces. Jim furnished some wonderful examples. We appreciate his contributions and willingness to proof our information.

Dennis Headrick was also a generous supporter. His collection provided some much-needed examples we were able to photograph. He also had many brochures and original advertising that were a terrific addition. Dennis also graciously read over our information. We thank him for his assistance and enthusiasm.

Walter Ludwig, curator of the Heisey Museum in Newark, Ohio, referred us to the museum web site and *Heisey News* for information about colors.

Dean Six could always be relied on for information. He is a longtime researcher of West Virginia glass, author of several glass books, Board Member of the West Virginia Museum of American Glass, and a researcher at Replacements. His valued knowledge is greatly appreciated and his enthusiasm and love of glass is felt by all who know him.

The following collectors and dealers provided some fine examples that were photographed at glass shows and we obtained more advertising information from them: Joanne, Janine & Dale Bender; Larry Hamilton, Bill Harmon, Robert Henicksman, Iris Natividad, Emily Osterman, Penny Renner, Wanda and Bill Rice, and Louise and Wayne Spears. All of you were so wonderful to share with us.

A note of thanks goes to the Pacific Northwest Fenton Association for enabling us to take photographs at their Spring and Fall shows. The Centralia Square Antique Mall in Centralia, Washington, and the Lafayette Schoolhouse Antique Mall in Lafayette, Oregon, generously let us photograph at their locations.

A special appreciation goes to the West Virginia Museum of American Glass located in Weston, West Virginia. This terrific group have worked hard to establish a museum where many fine examples of American glass can be seen by many. Their quest for glass company material is relentless, but more importantly their willingness to share information with anyone who requests it is exemplary. Information does no one any good unless it can be shared with all collectors. Much of the information available in this book is derived from their many acquisitions of catalogs, brochures, advertisements, correspondence, and monographs the museum has assembled. We appreciate their support of glass research.

PREFACE

Original Heisey postcard of the Heisey factory, dated on back, May 22, 1913
Note: In upper right corner: A. H. Heisey Glass Factory, Newark, Ohio

For several years, we were asked to write a book about Heisey glass. With so many books already available on the subject, it was hard to decide what direction to take. We wanted to contribute something that would educate new collectors to the subject yet be of benefit to advanced collectors as well. We sought lots of feedback with varied answers and learned that there was no current reference on Heisey's colors. While Heisey first made glass in crystal, they expanded their lines to make some of the finest colored glass available.

Many of the books available on Heisey glass utilize catalog reprints. While that was an excellent way to document the information, it did not convey the true colors of the glass. We therefore chose to define the colors that were produced and give a good sampling of the shapes and patterns that were made in each color. It is our hope that our photography portrays Heisey color as it looks in real life. Natural variations in some of the colors demonstrate the wonderful spectrum that can be found.

This work is not comprehensive of all the items made in each color, but rather a nice representative assortment.

Original photo of Heisey delivery truck, Circa 1930

Once you get a feeling for the color, you can recognize Heisey glass by the pattern or shape, even if it is not marked in the glass with the Heisey logo. Some Heisey colors show a wide array of variation and we address this by presenting different spectrums.

INTRODUCTION

The founder of Heisey glass was Augustus H. Heisey, who was born in Germany. His parents emigrated to the United States and settled near Merrittown, Pennsylvania. Augustus first learned about the glass trade in 1861, while he worked at Cascade Glass Works in Pittsburgh, Pennsylvania, which was operated by King, Son & Co.

When the American Civil War began, Augustus served with the U. S. Army 155th infantry. He fought at the Little Round Top in the Battle of Gettysburg.

After the war, Heisey worked as salesman for the Ripley Company. There he met, and later married, Susan Duncan, the daughter of George Duncan, one of the company's owners. George put his son, James, and his son-in-law, Augustus, in charge of the company a short time later and renamed it George Duncan and Sons, in 1874. Later, the company became part of the U. S. Glass

consolidation. Heisey gained further experience in the glass trade by serving on the new company's board of directors. Having his own glass company was never far from his mind. Finally, in 1893, he left to do something for himself. Construction began on his own factory in Newark, Ohio, in 1895. Problems delayed the completion until 1896. He called his business A. H. Heisey & Company.

Augustus Heisey believed that Crystal glass best conveyed design patterns on the glass. When A. H. Heisey & Company opened in 1896, only clear glass was made in a variety of patterns. Emerald, Ivorina Verde, and Opal colors were introduced a short time later, but was issued only in limited amounts perhaps because of pressure from competition with the U.S. Glass and Northwood companies.

Original Heisey postcard of the Heisey factory, dated on back, December 13, 1910
Note: In upper left corner: Newark, Ohio A. H. Heisey & Co.

Original Heisey "Quality, Durability Style Heisey Crystal" round multi color label

Crystal glass continued to be the mainstay of Heisey production. Only after much prodding by his oldest son, George, and other employees, who saw that colored glass was selling well for other glass companies, was some color added to the Heisey lines. By the 1920s, the age of color was here to stay. Yet Heisey continued to produce their Crystal lines the entire time they were making glassware. Augustus may have believed the public would again be attracted to clear crystal. But colored glass took root with the public, even during the 1930s, and there was continually more demand for it.

THE HEISEY TRADEMARK

The Heisey company was one of the first in America to develop a special embossed trademark for their glass. The idea came from Augustus' son, George, who used the design of his fraternity pin as a model. The "H" inside a diamond was adopted in 1900 and trademarked a year later. Thereafter, their advertisements stated that their glass was marked with a distinctive "Diamond H" logo. Of all the embossed marks on glass, one would have to agree that Heisey's Diamond H logo is the most recognized one by glass enthusiasts today.

Early mark of June 21, 1908 Patented Diamond H

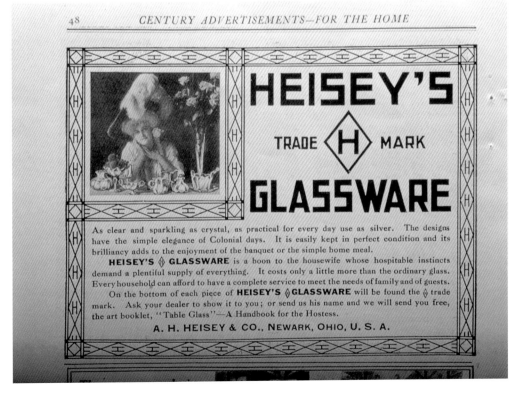

Original Heisey advertising for their trademark glassware from National Geographic September 1911

Beginning glass collectors have thought all Heisey glass should be marked with the logo in the glass, but that is not exactly so. While many pieces were marked in the glass, others had a paper label stating that they were made by Heisey. Of course, through the years the paper labels would get washed off the item and then would no longer be marked. Heisey wanted to indicate that there was no substitute for their product. By finding the Heisey trademark, the public would be assured of the best quality. Today, collectors can educate themselves to recognize the Heisey patterns

Original Heisey label, Patent Applied For, Heisey's

Original Heisey label, Patented, Heisey's

Original Heisey label, A H Heisey & Company Inc. Newark, Ohio USA Trademark H

Original labels
Left: Heisey Diamond H; **Right**: Heisey's Diamond H

VISIBLE COOKING WARE

One of Heisey's most interesting designs was stopped almost as soon as it was created. In 1919, Heisey developed a special, oven-proof cooking ware and applied for a patent. The cookware was given the name Visible Cooking Ware, which Heisey listed as having a high polish and being non-staining. Around the same time, The Corning Glass Company, of Corning, New York, developed their own oven-proof glass, called Pyrex, and was not anxious for another company to have products similar to theirs. They sued Heisey for infringement and Heisey immediately dropped the project. Both the Fry and the Mckee glass companies worked with Corning to develop their own bake ware: Corning issued Fry a license in 1920 to make glass under the name of Fry Oven Glass, and issued McKee a license in 1921 to make their bake ware line called "Glassbake." Why Heisey dropped the project so easily and didn't work with Corning is not known. Before it dropped the Visible Cooking Ware line, however, Heisey had already listed 45 pieces they intended to make. There were to be different sizes of casseroles and baking dishes. Only a few pieces were actually made before the lawsuit was filed, and they are exceedingly rare today.

The majority of Visible Cooking Ware pieces are found in a pale yellow green color called Vaseline. Since no formula relating to this glassware has been found, one must assume the basic formula was a version of Canary, with other ingredients added to make the glass oven-proof. A few pieces were also listed as made in Crystal. All of the Visible Cooking Ware pieces have the Diamond H logo on them. Any Heisey oven-proof pieces are treasures when found on the secondary market today.

Original Heisey trademark of Visible Cooking Ware

Augustus Heisey's son, Wilson Heisey, was a chemistry major in school and had been involved with the development of glass formulas. Emmet Olson was a glass specialist hired by Heisey in 1919 to make sure the stoppers of cruets and decanters fit properly. The two men worked together on designing formulas.

When Augustus Heisey died in 1922, Wilson Heisey became the new company president and Emmet Olson became the company's chemist. Color was almost immediately added to the Heisey line, since Wilson was so interested in its development

Emmet Olson kept very precise notes on formulas. His lists of color ingredients were compiled, along with observations in variations of colors, costs of making glass, and other glass company formulas. He obtained glass formulas from many sources. He worked very closely with R. R. Shively of Drakenfeld & Co. to develop many of the glass formulas used at Heisey. Olson's correspondence also reveals information exchanged with George Blumenthal of Crown Chemical, H. L. Haney of Harshaw Chemical, and Henry Harrington of Allied Chemical & Dye.

In the late 1920s and through the Depression years, Heisey developed several colors that were well received by the public. When Prohibition was repealed in the United States in 1933, Heisey expanded their lines to include attractive bar ware to produce added sales. This glassware is frequently known as "repeal" glass.

GLASS CUTTING

Heisey opened the company's glass-cutting shop around 1914. Various cuttings were tried and exhibited at trade shows, but if they were not well received the cutting was not put into production. The earliest cuttings were primarily put on baskets. Little is known about the early cutting designers, but in 1933 Emil Krall was hired to cut glass, along with several members of his family. He had been a special cutter for the Austrian court and his expertise was well known in Europe among prestigious families. With threat of another major war brewing in Europe, Krall fled to the United States for safety, and Heisey welcomed his talent to their cutting shop.

Krall's style was to create elaborate and intricate patterns that gave the feeling of movement. To publicize Krall's work, Heisey sent him to special department stores to demonstrate how a cutting was achieved. Radio interviews gave listeners his background in a family of cutters with connections to the Austrian court and European royal families. This highlighted the special cuttings that were being done at Heisey and generated more sales.

When Krall left the Heisey company in 1941 to pursue his own interests, his brother, Willibald, assumed Emil's position as Heisey's head designer. Emil's two sons and Willibald's son also worked in the cutting shop. Cuttings continued to be done until the company closed in 1958.

With talent, a steady hand, and an eye for detail, designers make cuttings one of the most personal ways that glassware can be made distinctive. Anyone who has watched a cutter at work can imagine some of those wonderful old cuttings being applied across the face of a piece of glass. Heisey also developed many etching patterns, such as their most famous patterns, Orchid and Rose, that are the most recognized by the public today.

THE 1940s

The glass world changed with the onset of World War II. A shortage of chemicals needed for glass colors caused Heisey to make only Crystal glass in the mid-1940s. Many decorating companies purchased Heisey's clear blanks and decorated them with painted or flashed colors, in the hope of filling the void in the colored glassware market. The U. S. government had frozen prices during the war. One way around their restrictions was to decorate clear glass. It was less expensive to flash ruby on than to make solid ruby glassware, yet the ruby price could be charged in accordance with the government guidelines. Using metal ormolu with the glass was another way companies made their glassware more desirable. Some glass companies purchased the metal ormolu, but more commonly metal companies purchased the glass.

Royal Hickman, a former designer at the Royal Haeger Pottery, came to work for Heisey in 1941. He designed many of the Heisey animals. When Tennessee William's play, *The Glass Menagerie* was on Broadway in 1946, glass animals from Heisey were prominently displayed on the stage. Later, when the play was made into a movie in 1950, Heisey animals were used again. A famous Heisey advertisement of the time featured actress Jane Wyman surrounded by Heisey animals. This was a good marketing campaign that department stores could benefit from to encourage their customers to buy a favorite animal that was featured in the movie.

The unfortunate death of Wilson Heisey, in 1942, contributed to some of the problems of the company. T. Clarence became the new president and took control of the company during this difficult period. When the end of the war came, Heisey struggled to compete in the marketplace, like so many of the other great American glass companies. Cheap glass imports flooded United States markets and the glass worker's union demanded an increase in wages that had been frozen during the war. Heisey replied by designing new patterns and colors.

THE 1950s

Eva Zeisel, a famous products designer, was hired in 1954 to develop new lines of glass for Heisey. A contract was made with Holophane, in 1955, to make Verlys moulds in Heisey colors. Sadly, neither agreement produced increases in sales. In the end, nothing seemed to help.

In December of 1957, the company closed for the Christmas holiday as usual. But the Heisey management and family members decided not to reopen the company after evaluating their finances. Employees were greatly surprised when the company did not reopen in January. Not only were the employees and their families affected but the economy of the entire community was devastated. Finally, in 1958, the Heisey glass company was sold to the Imperial Company, including all the accounts, moulds, and trademarks. A long and distinguished era of Heisey glassmaking had concluded. It is sad to think of what they might have achieved.

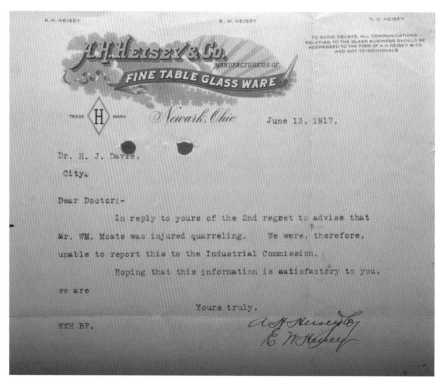

Original Heisey letter dated June 13, 1917 to Dr. H. J. Davis about Wm. Moats and signed by E. N. Heisey

Original Heisey postcard of the Heisey factory, dated on back
October 11, 1917
Upper right corner: 32 A. H. Heisey & Co.'s Plant, Newark, Ohio

Original Heisey large envelope with return address that advertising brochures were sent in.

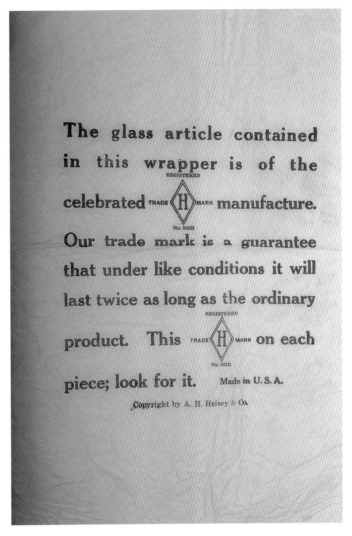

Original Heisey tissue that glassware was wrapped in after purchasing at fine department stores.

Heisey store display sign that is Black and Mirrored

Original Common Capital stock certificate #186 for shares in the amount of $100 each

Original Preferred Capital stock certificate #108 for shares in the amount of $100 each

Original Heisey checks: **Top**: Check made out to Collector of Internal Revenue, October 28, 1948, $4889.08
Bottom: Check made out to B. & O. R. R. Co., June 28, 1951, $26.76

Original Heisey order blank #358797

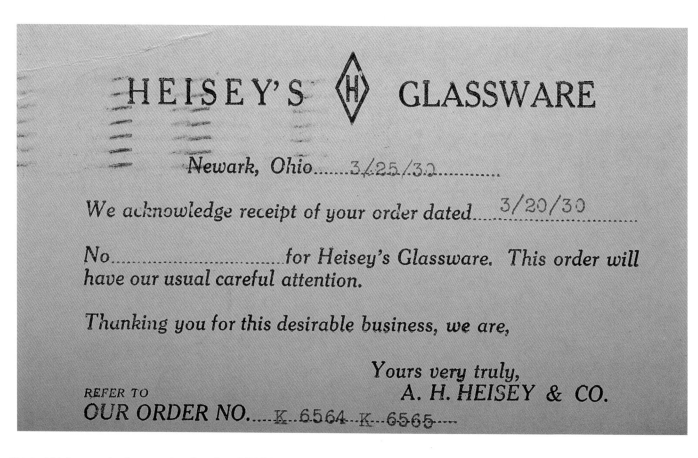

Original Heisey receipt for an order placed on 3/20/30.

Original Heisey payroll check for Desso Nichols in the amount of $38.06. This employee worked in the batch mixing room at Heisey. The date on the check, December 24, 1957, was the last day the Heisey factory operated.

Original Heisey book of matches: "Glassware of this label should be on every table." Produced for Heisey by Ohio Match Co, Wadsworth, Ohio

Original postcard showing Easter on the Boardwalk, Atlantic City, N. J. The Heisey billboard sign is in the upper left background.

Original Heisey store display sign in Crystal

1. THE COLORS OF HEISEY

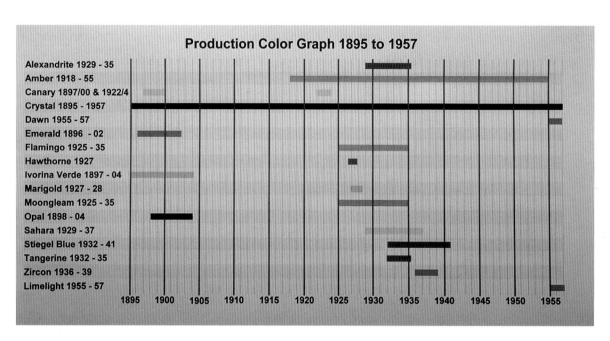

Graph of colors and production dates

Production Color Graph 1895 to 1957

Alexandrite 1929 - 35
Amber 1918 - 55
Canary 1897/00 & 1922/4
Crystal 1895 - 1957
Dawn 1955 - 57
Emerald 1896 - 02
Flamingo 1925 - 35
Hawthorne 1927
Ivorina Verde 1897 - 04
Marigold 1927 - 28
Moongleam 1925 - 35
Opal 1898 - 04
Sahara 1929 - 37
Stiegel Blue 1932 - 41
Tangerine 1932 - 35
Zircon 1936 - 39
Limelight 1955 - 57

1895 1900 1905 1910 1915 1920 1925 1930 1935 1940 1945 1950 1955

Original Heisey booklet, "Gifts of Glassware", title page, 1928

All of the colors that Heisey produced are explored in alphabetical order on the following pages. There were sixteen regular production colors: Alexandrite, Amber, Canary, Crystal, Dawn, Emerald, Flamingo, Hawthorne, Ivorina Verde, Ivory, Marigold, Moongleam, Opal, Sahara, Stiegel Blue, Tangerine and Zircon/Limelight. After the regular colors, the experimental colors will be listed. Each color is defined and dates of production are given in a sampling of patterns and shapes. The final chapter will explore the wide variety of decorating that took place from outside decorating companies.

The captions include the Color, Pattern Name, Pattern Number, Measurements, and Value.

ALEXANDRITE

The Heisey Company introduced their version of Alexandrite, in 1929 and produced it until 1935. It is assumed that Heisey obtained this formula from an European associate and possibly directly from Moser. This color very closely imitates the natural stone of the same name. It is a light transparent pink lavender with a hint of blue that changes color under different types of lighting. This dichroic color looks more lavender or pink with a light ruby tint under incandescent or natural light. When this special glass is shown under fluorescent light it takes on the bluish green tones that are very distinctive. The formula contains the rare earth element of Neodymium. With the failure of the Hawthorne color, it was hoped the public would embrace this new color. It was immediately popular and sold very well for Heisey. Since it was expensive to make, the Alexandrite was priced higher. Today, the Alexandrite still commands a premium price.

The Moser Art Glass Company located in Carlsbad, Czechoslovakia first perfected the Alexandrite color in the early 1920s. Their German chemist in 1920 began experimenting with the addition of rare earth elements into various glass formulas. This led Moser to develop brand new, breathtaking types of glassware in 1922. Their Alexandrit and Alexandritbleis colors, which were lead based, have in their formula approximately 4 to 5% of the neodymium oxide. Since this glass changes color under different types of lighting, Moser was able to capitalize on this characteristic at the 1925 International Exhibition of Decorative Arts. They used various examples of lighting to bring out the intensity and beauty of this new color. This event was held in Paris and there was lots of competition. A prestigious gold medal was awarded to Moser for their use of this unique glass. Leo Moser assisted with the development of this color. The Alexandrit name was actually acid stamped or engraved on the base of a few items and is considered very rare.

Moser developed a total of 15 different rare-earth glass formulas. Other than the Alexandrit color, these special formulas remained unique to the glass world.

As a special historical note, when Hitler was invading Europe and executing Jewish people, the Moser family was frantically trying to escape his persecution. Eleanor Roosevelt intervened and obtained passports for them to the United States, where they remained until the end of the war.

Other glass companies produced their own versions of this color. Cambridge produced a color they called *Heatherbloom* and Fostoria developed a color called *Wisteria*. Tiffin's color was called *Twilight*. Each of these colors is dichroic and will appear to change colors under different types of lighting.

Alexandrite, Vase, 8.75" tall, 11" wide, multi faceted cut, Made by Moser, engraved mark of: Alexandrite Moser Carlsbad, **$2500**

Original advertising: "Rare Colors to Inspire the Hostess Today". from Good Housekeeping, June 1930. Colors represented were: Alexandrite and Sahara

Alexandrite, Trident #134, Oval Bowl, 14" long, 7.75" wide, 1930 to 1935, **$650**

Alexandrite, Trident #134, Duo candlestick, 5.75" tall, 6.5" wide, 1930 to 1935, **$250**

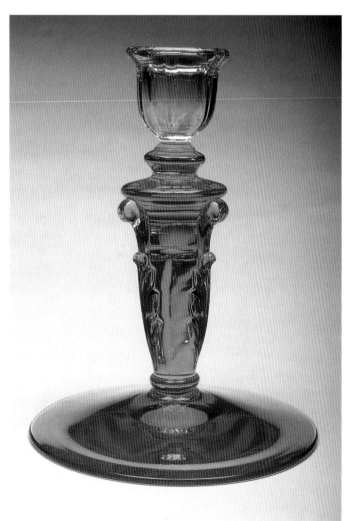

Alexandrite, #1000, Paneled Marmalade jar, 5" tall, 1929 to 1935, **$950**

Alexandrite, Empress #135, Candlestick, 6.5" tall, 1929 to 1935, **$300**

Alexandrite, Empress #1401, Bowl with dolphin feet, 11" wide, 1929 to 1935, **$395**

Advertising "Lilies of France inspired the design of this lovely glass" from National Geographic September 1930

Alexandrite, Empress #1401, Candlestick, 6" tall, dolphin feet, 1929 to 1935, **$400**

Alexandrite, Empress #1401, Cup and saucer; coffee cup, 2.6" tall, saucer, 6.5" wide, 1929 to 1935, **$125**

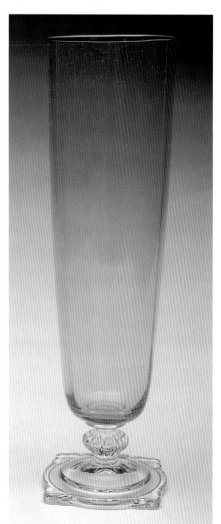

Alexandrite, Carcassone #3390, pilsner, 9.5" tall, Crystal base, 1930 to 1935, **$145**

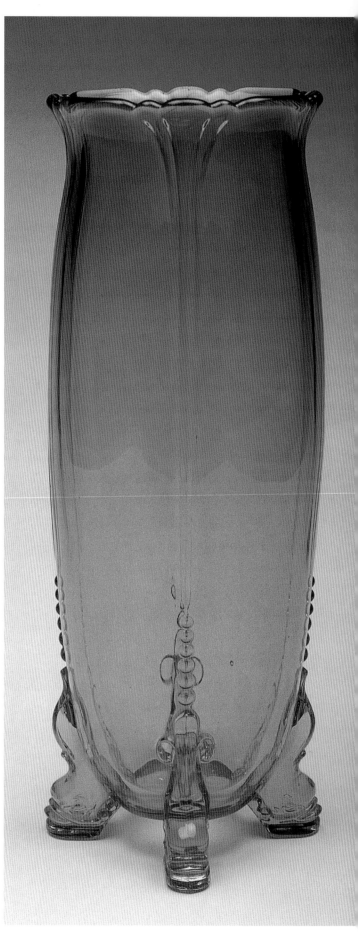

Alexandrite, Empress #1401, Vase, 9.5" tall, dolphin feet, 1929 to 1935, **$350**

Alexandrite, Ball #4045,
Wide optic, Vases, 1935
Top: 8.5" tall, **$1900**
Bottom Left: 6.5" tall,
$900; **Center**: 3.75"
tall, **$375**; **Right**: 5.5"
tall, **$750**

Left:
Alexandrite, Janice
#4220, Vase, 7" tall,
1930 to 1935, **$650**

Amber

Amber was introduced about 1918 and was listed as late as 1955 in Olson's formula notebook. There were actually nine different Amber formulas listed in this notebook: *Amber*, two for *Selenium Amber*, two for *Lead Amber*, *New Experimental Amber*, two for *Cotton Amber*, and *Amber for Fred Harvey*. Some of the early pieces of *Amber* were made as bar ware and table ware for the Fred Harvey Restaurants. Throughout Heisey's life, *Amber* was produced periodically as orders came in. The dark version of *Amber* was referred to as *Sultana* and introduced around 1951. This color was produced for a very short time. The light color of *Amber* was called *Honey Amber* by collectors. The spectrum of Amber from light to dark would at times make you think that you are looking at different colors and not just a variation of one color. In knowing that different formulas of *Amber* existed, you understand why there are different tints. This accounts for the names given to the far ends of the spectrum of this color.

All of the major glass companies had some type of *Amber* color, with some lighter and darker than those Heisey developed.

Right:
Amber (Sultana - Dark Amber),
Doe Head #1, 6" tall, 3.5"
wide, Designed by Royal
Hickman, 1947 to 1949,
$2950

Amber, Elephants, 1944 to 1955
Left: Large #1, 4.8" tall, 6.5" long, **$3000**;
Right: Medium #2, 4" tall, 6.5" long, **$2400**

Amber, Flying Mare #1, 8.75" tall, 11.5" long, Designed by Royal
Hickman, 1951 to 1952
Left: Honey Amber, **$6000**; **Right**: Sultana, **$5500**

Left: Sultana (Dark Amber), Filly #2,, 8.75" tall, 5" long, 1948 to 1949, **$4000**
Center: Amber, Elephant mug #1591A, 5" tall, 5" wide, holds 12 ounces, 1952, **$650**
Right: Honey Amber (light amber), Plug Horse #1540, 4.25" tall, 3.6" long, 1941 to 1946, **$375**

Amber, Fish, Tropical #101, 12.5" tall, 5.75" wide, Designed by Royal Hickman, 1948 to 1949, **$3800**

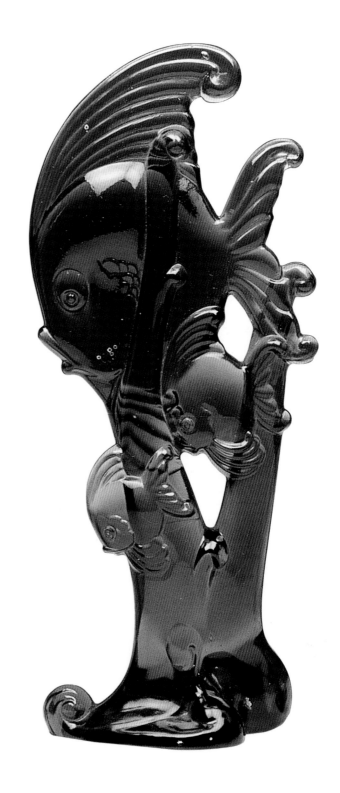

Amber, Asiatic Pheasant #100, 10" tall, 7.25" long, Designed by Royal Hickman, 1945 to 1955, **$850**

Amber, Dolphin Candlestick #110, 10.25" tall, 4.25" wide, 1925 to 1935, **$1000**

Amber, #201, Tumbler, 4" tall, Made for Fred Harvey Restaurants, 1950s, **$60**

Amber, #1125, Plate, 7.5" wide, Made for Fred Harvey Restaurants, 1950s, **$45**

Amber, Medium Flat Panel #353, Soda tumbler, 5.5" tall, 10-ounce, Made for Fred Harvey Restaurants, 1950s, **$95**

Amber, Yeoman #1184, Water goblet, 6" tall, 1935 to 1957, **$95**

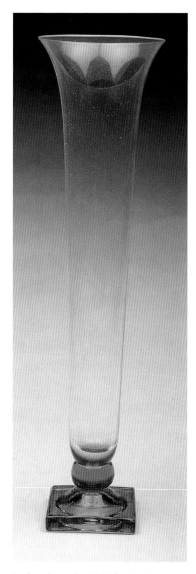

Amber footed, #5012, Bud vase, 10" vase, 1943, **$125**

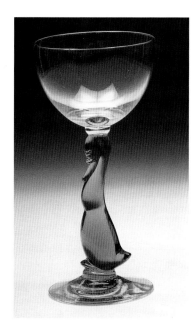

Amber, Goose Stem #5058, Sherbet, 5.75" tall, 1948, **$475**

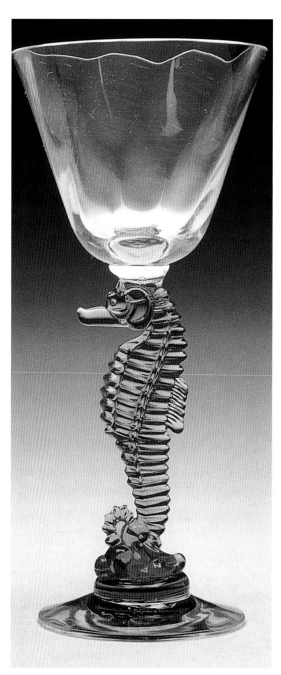

Amber (Sultana), Seahorse #5074 stem, 6.75" tall, 1950, **$1000+**

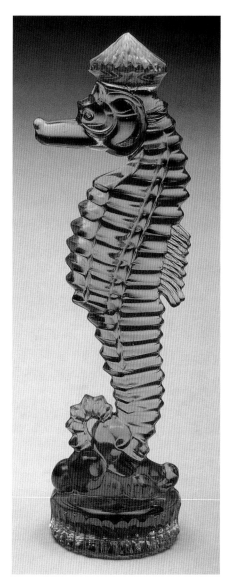

Amber, Sea Horse #5074, 4.5" tall, whimsey, 1950, **$1250**

Amber stem, Legionnaire #5077, Cocktail, 3.75" tall, 3.5 ounce, 1950 to 1957, **$35**

CANARY

Canary was introduced around 1897 and was very intense. This color has the qualities of both yellow and green. Collectors have also called this color *Vaseline*. The basic definition of Vaseline states that all Vaseline will fluoresce under a black light, but all glass that fluoresces is not Vaseline. To be *Canary* or *Vaseline* it must show both yellow and green colors when it is not under a black light. This color fits the basic definition well. It contains Uranium Oxide and will fluoresce under a black light. Items in this color do not turn up very often and normally are expensive. Pieces initially issued are in the patterns of Locket on Chain and Winged Scroll. *Canary* was reissued again in 1922, but the formula was altered. These later pieces will be paler and do not have such an intensity as the original color. Patterns in this later version were Cross Line Flute, Narrow Flute with Rim, Priscilla, and Recessed Panel.

Other glass companies produced this type of color and it was known as *Vaseline*. Fostoria and Tiffin, like Heisey, gave their Vaseline color the name *Canary*. Fenton gave this color the name *Topaz* for their glass lines.

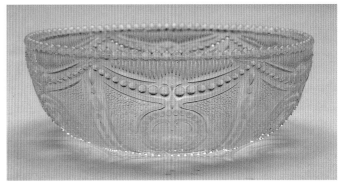

Canary, Locket on Chain #160, Bowl, 4" wide, ice cream nappy, 1898, **$275**

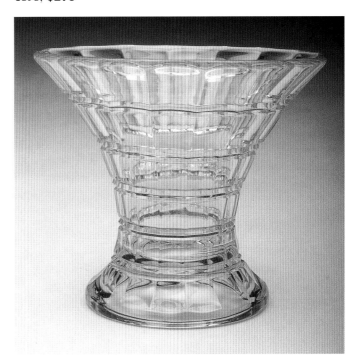

Canary, Cross Lined Flute #451, Vase, 5.25" tall, 1914 to 1920, **$300**

Canary, Pinwheel and Fan #350, Bowl, 8.5" wide, 1910, **$800**

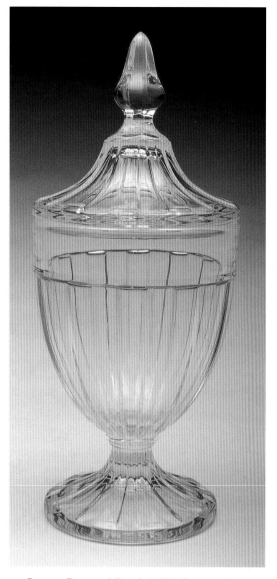

Canary, Yeoman #1184, Bouillon bowl, 2.5" tall, 4" wide, 1913 to 1920, **$90**

Canary, Recessed Panel #465, Covered Candy, 9" tall, 4" wide, 1915 to 1920, **$1450**

Canary, Narrow Flute With Rim #473, Oval plate, 6.75" long, 1916 to 1920, **$200**

Canary, Inside Scallop #1192, Bowl, 9.5" wide, 1923, **$450**

CRYSTAL

Crystal was the first color of glass produced and the only color of glass that founder Augustus H. Heisey really liked. He thought the *Crystal* color reveals the true pattern and design of the glass and to be more popular for use since it works well with any type of decoration. He thought that if Heisey only produced *Crystal*, that the public would have to embrace it and only shop at Heisey. That thought certainly did not hold up, and Heisey needed to produce colored ware to compete in the marketplace. Only *Crystal* and *Amber* were produced during World War II, since it was difficult to obtain the necessary ingredients for colored glass. *Crystal* was still being made when Heisey closed in 1958.

Crystal was also a mainstay at all of the other glass companies, but not as significantly as it was at Heisey.

Sometimes pieces of *Crystal* have been sun colored, to give them a light to dark amethyst color. This was not ever a Heisey color and should not be treated as such. Most Heisey collectors do not find sun colored *Crystal* attractive. However, the collectors of sun colored glassware are quite enamored with many pieces. Sometimes, a few of the sun colored items can be confused with the *Hawthorne* color. Uniformity of color and not matching any Heisey color are your best clues for identifying sun colored pieces.

Advertising for the Glass Menagerie, a Broadway play from Tennessee Williams from Life magazine 1946. Actress Julie Haydon was surrounded by crystal animals, of which many were Heisey.

Crystal, Clydesdale #2, 7.5" tall, 6.75" long, 1942 to 1948, **$550**

Crystal, Goose #2, Wings halfway up, 4.6" tall, 8.5" long, 1942 to 1955, **$145**

Crystal, Elephants, 1944 to 1955
Top: Small #3, 4.5" tall, 4.75" long, **$295**
Bottom Left: Large #1, 4.75" tall, 6.5" long, **$495**;
Bottom Right: Medium #2, 4" tall, 6.5" long, **$375**

Crystal, Pheasant, Asiatic #100, 10" tall, 7.25" long, 1945 to 1955, **$475**

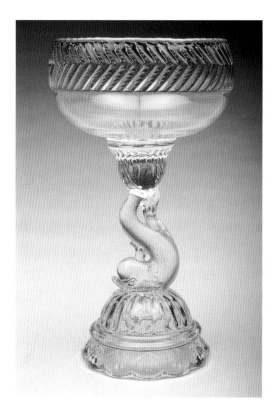

Crystal, Petticoat Dolphin #109, Comport, 9.25" tall, 5" wide, 1925 to 1935, **$195**

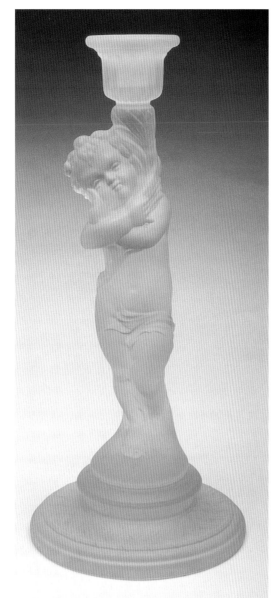

Crystal, Cherub #111,
Candlestick, 11.5" tall,
satin finish, 1926 to
1929, **$275**

Crystal, Banded Flute #150,
Shaker, 3.25" tall, with
sanitary top (metal top with
glass duster), 1907 to 1932,
$35

Original Heisey booklet,
"Gifts of Glassware",
page 22, Glassware of
Rich Distinction,
showing Diamond
Optic and candelabra
with colored prisms

Crystal, Old Williamsburg
#300-0, Candelabra, 9.5" tall,
Stiegel Blue bobeche and
prisms, 1932 to 1941, **$295**

Crystal, Paneled Cane #315, Covered Butter, 5" tall, 7.5" wide, 1901 to 1906, **$125**

Crystal, Pillows #325, Covered Mustard, 4.5" tall, 1901 to 1910, **$180**

Crystal, Paneled Cane #315, 1901 to 1906
Left: Covered Sugar, 6.5" tall, **$70**; **Right**: Creamer, 4.5" tall, **$50**

Crystal, Prince of Wales #335, 1902 to 1912
Left: Cruet, 7" tall, **$195**; **Center**: Sherbet, 4" tall, **$35**; **Right**: Pitcher, 8.75" tall, 1/2 gallon, **$200**

Crystal, Prince of Wales #335, 1902 to 1912
Left: Covered Sugar, 7" tall, **$75**; **Right**: Creamer, 5.25" tall, **$55**

Crystal, Continental #339, 1903 to 1910
Left to Right: Celery Vase, 5.75" tall, **$65**; Goblet, 6.25" tall, **$32**; Pitcher, 9.25" tall, **$165**; Wine Goblet, 4.25" tall, **$35**

Crystal, Sunburst #343, Pitcher, 7.75" tall, three quart, 1903 to 1913, **$295**

Crystal, Medium Flat Panel #353, Covered Marmalade Jar, 5.5" tall, 3.25" wide, 1909-1929, **$50**

Crystal, Sunburst #343, 1903 to 1912
Left: Covered Sugar, 7" tall, **$75**;
Right: Creamer, 5" tall, **$55**

Advertising of
Heisey's Glassware
from Good House-
keeping May 1913

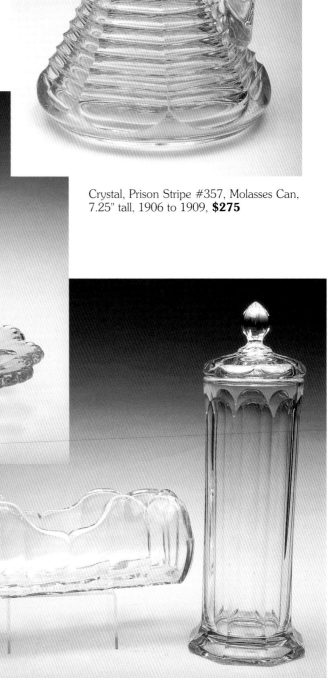

Crystal, Prison Stripe #357, Molasses Can,
7.25" tall, 1906 to 1909, **$275**

Crystal, Prison Stripe #357, Covered Butter, 5.5"
tall, 7.5" wide, 1906, **$145**

Crystal, Straw holders
Left: Medium Flat Panel #353, Sanitary Straw
tray, 9.75" long, 3.5" tall, 1905 to 1909, **$295**;
Right: Colonial Panel #331,12.5" tall, 3.5" wide,
Covered, 1907 to 1929, **$400**

Crystal, Queen Anne #365, Covered Butter, 5.75" tall, 8" wide, 1907 to 1913, **$200**

Crystal, Colonial Scalloped Top #400, Punch bowl, 6.75" tall, 15.5" wide, Base, 5.5" tall, 9.5" wide, Overall height 12", 1909 to 1924, **$350**

Crystal, Narrow Flute #394, Pitchers, 1910
Left: 4.75" tall, one pint, **$55**; **Right**: 7" tall, 1/2 gallon, **$125**

Below:
Crystal, Raised Loop #439, 1910 to 1913
Left: Sugar, 6.5" wide, **$100**;
Right: Creamer, 4.75" wide, **$100**

Crystal, Daisy and Leaves #427, 1911
Left: Sugar, 2.75" tall, **$55**; **Right**: Creamer, 3.5" tall, **$50**;

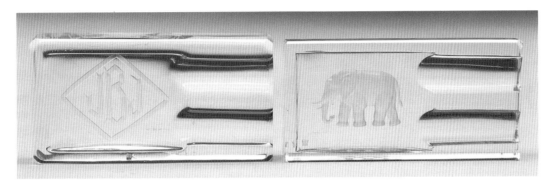

Crystal, Fatima #439, ashtray, 1923 to 1937
Left: Monogrammed JBJ, .5" tall, 1.6" wide, 3" long **$35**; **Right**: Czechoslovakia copy with intaglio cutting of an elephant; mark in bottom corner is a eagle or butterfly, .65" tall, 1.5" wide, 3.1" long, heavier weight, **Note**: Shown only for comparison

Advertising of Heisey's Glassware from Atlantic Monthly 1914

Crystal, Colonial Cupped
Scallop #397, Gold trim,
1912 to 1913
Left: Sugar, 2.75" tall, **$60**;
Right: Creamer, 3" tall,
$40

Below:
Crystal, Convex Circle #461 1/2, 1915
Left: Pitcher, 6.5" tall, three pint, **$325**;
Center: Spooner, 6.8" tall, **$175**; **Right**:
Crushed Fruit, 10" tall, 6" wide, **$400**

Crystal, Harding #1022,
Windsor Heisey cutting,
1921 to 1933
Left: Covered Sugar, 4.5"
tall, **$70**; **Right**: Creamer,
3.25" tall, **$50**

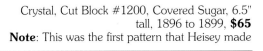

Crystal, Cut Block #1200, Covered Sugar, 6.5"
tall, 1896 to 1899, **$65**
Note: This was the first pattern that Heisey made

Crystal, Fandango #1201, Covered Horseradish, 4.25" tall, 1896
to 1903, **$70**

Crystal, Beaded Panel and Sunburst #1235, 1897 to 1913
Left: Covered Sugar, 6" tall, **$75**; **Right**: Creamer, 4.5" tall, **$55**

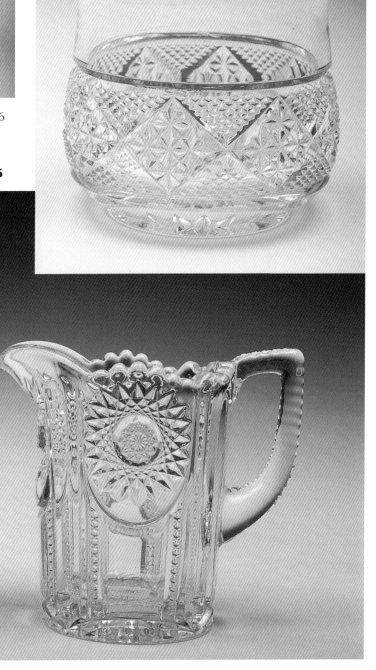

Crystal, Twist #1252,
1928 to 1937
Left: Covered Sugar,
3.75" tall, **$50**; **Right**:
Creamer, 2.5" tall, **$35**

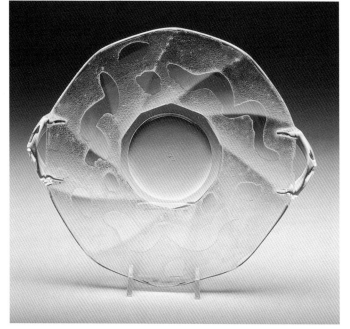

Crystal, Twist #1252,
Lemon plate, 6.75" wide,
Arctic etching #9009,
1928 to 1937, **$24**

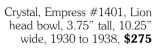

Crystal, Empress #1401, Lion
head bowl, 3.75" tall, 10.25"
wide, 1930 to 1938, **$275**

Crystal, Empress #1401, Covered Candy, 6" tall, 6.25" wide,
Antarctic etching #454, 1930 to 1938, **$110**

Crystal, Aristocrat #1430, Covered
candy, 13.5" tall, 3.5" wide, Riviere
#794 cutting, Heisey cutting shop,
1933 to 1937, **$500**

Crystal, Empress #1401, Plate,
11" wide, Krall cutting, 1930 to
1938, **$125**

Heisey brochure advertising
Stanhope

Crystal, Stanhope #1483, Plaskon
handle, 1936 to 1941
Top: Blue Handle, Frosted accents, Sugar,
3.25" tall, **$80**; Creamer, 4" tall, **$60**
Bottom Left: Red Handle, Creamer, 4"
tall, **$45**; Sugar, 3.25" tall, **$60**; **Bottom
Right**: Black Handle, Sugar, 3.25" tall,
$50; Creamer, 4" tall, **$40**

Crystal, World #1493,
Duo candlestick, 6.5"
tall, 10" long, 1937 to
1938, **$395**

Crystal, Ridgeleigh #1469, 1935 to 1944
Top Row: Left: Creamer, Hotel, 3.75" tall, flat, **$45**; **Center**: Marmalade with cover, 4.75" tall, **$60**; **Right**: Comport with cover, 6" tall, **$60**
Center Row: Left: Sugar, Hotel, 3.6" tall, flat, **$45**; **Center**: Lemon dish with cover, 5" wide, **$60**; **Right**: Shaker, 3" tall, flat, **$20**
Bottom Row: Left: Ashtray, 3.4" wide, heart, **$18**; **Center Left**: Ashtray, 3.25" wide, club, **$18**; **Center Right**: Ashtray, 3.75" wide, **$18**; **Right**: Ashtray, 3.25" wide, **$18**

Crystal, Ridgeleigh #1469, 1935 to 1944
Top: Bowl, 14" long, swan handled, **$450**
Center Row: Left: Cigarette box, 3.75" long, **$45**; **Center**: Cigarette box with chrome lid and dolphin finial, 5.75" long, **$35**; **Right**: Ice Tub, 4.6" tall, tab handles, **$95**
Bottom Row: Left: Cigarette jar, 3.75" tall, **$65**; **Center Left**: Cocktail rest and coaster, 3.25" wide, **$65**; **Center Right**: Bowl, dessert, 4.5" wide, with 6" liner, **$45**; **Right**: Ashtray, 5" oval with cigarette holder, 2" holder, **$65**

Crystal, Horse head ashtray #1489, 3" tall, 4.5" long, 1944 to 1945, **$75**

Crystal, Crystolite #1503, Candy Box, 6.9" wide, brass plated lid, glass flower finial, 1938 to 1957, **$75**

Crystal, Crystolite #1503, 1938 to 1957
Top Row: Left: Candlestick, two light, 5.75" tall, **$45**; **Center**: Candle block, one light, 2" tall, **$24**; **Right**: Candlestick, three light, 3.8" tall, **$38**
Bottom Row: Left: Candle block, one light, 2.4" tall, **$30**; **Center Left**: Candle block, one light, 2" tall, rosette, **$12**; **Center Right**: Hurricane candle block, 2.5" wide, **$35**; **Right**: Candle block, one light, 1.8" wide, square rosette, **$20**

Crystal, Crystolite #1503, 1938 to 1957
Top Row: Left: Plate, coupe, 7.3" wide, **$35**; **Right**: Comport, 5.1" tall, oval two spout, **$45**
Bottom Row: Left: Cup and saucer, coffee, **$18**; **Center**: Tumbler, footed, 4.8" tall, juice, **$35**; **Right**: Bowl, Touraine, 8.5" wide, **$85**

Crystal, Crystolite #1503, water pitchers, 1938 to 1957
Left: Blown, flat, 8.25" tall, 64 ounces, **$150**; **Right**: Swan handled, 64 ounces, **$795**

WHIRLPOOL

As surely as the clear, cool rippling mountain streams, eddies and whirlpools draw us to them irresistibly — so Heisey's new sparkling WHIRLPOOL pattern calls enticingly.

WHIRLPOOL design has caught the spirit of yesteryear and offers special appeal to those who do not only love to surround themselves with the atmosphere of the early pioneers but who insist on that touch of practicability so essential in this modern world of ours.

Pieces in the WHIRLPOOL line are offered at prices as attractive as the design itself; serving to make this new creation in glass available to every home in which genuine beauty is appreciated.

NO-1506

WHIRL·POOL a new HEISEY creation

Patent Applied for.

Original Heisey brochure advertising Whirlpool

Crystal, Whirlpool #1506, Covered Mustard, 4.25" tall, 1938 to 1957, **$145**

Crystal, Waverly #1519, Cigarette jar with cover 5.1" tall, 3.75" wide, Orchid etching #507, sea horse handled, 1940 to 1957, **$195**

Original advertising: "Heisey Rose...Romance Etched in Crystal", from House Beautiful December 1949

Crystal, Elephant mug #1519, 5" tall, 5" wide, holds 12 ounces, 1952, **$300**

Crystal, Rose etching #515, 1949 to 1957
Back row, Left to right: Waverly #1519, Relish, 11.25" long, oblong, two equal outside sections and celery center section, **$98**; Cup, 2.5" tall, 6 ounces and saucer, 6" wide, **$48**
Front Row, Left to right: Store display sign, 3.25" tall, 3.25" wide, **$350**; Queen Anne #1509, Jelly bowl, 6" wide, 4 toed, **$48**

Crystal, Military Hat #1536, ashtray. 1.2" tall, 3.5" long, 1941 to 1947
Left: Cutting, **$60**; **Right**: Plain, **$40**

Original Heisey brochure
advertising Lariat

Crystal, Lariat #1540, baskets, 1941 to 1957
Left: Footed, loop stem, 8.5" tall, **$145**;
Center: Flat, oval, 8.25 long, **$115**; **Right**:
Footed, one ball stem, graduated loops on
sides, 10" tall, **$225**

Crystal, Lariat #1540, Bowl, horse head feet, 8.5" wide, 1945, **Market price undetermined**

Crystal, Lariat #1540, Covered Candy, 7" tall, 6" wide, Moonglo cutting #980, 1941 to 1957, **$125**

Crystal, Plug horse #1540, 4.25" tall, 3.5" long, 1941 to 1946, **$100**

Original Heisey Athena label

Original Heisey brochure advertising Plantation

Original Advertising: Plantation, from House Beautiful December 1948

Crystal, Athena #1541, Covered Candy, 5" tall, 5.5" wide, 1943 to 1948, **$75**

Crystal, Plantation #1567, 1948 to 1957
Back Left: Bridge tray, 8" round, two sections, indent for cup, **$150**; **Back Right**: Relish, 13.5" long, oval, 4 equal outside sections and center celery section, **$60**;
Center: Creamer and sugar, footed, on oval 8.5" tray, **$125**
Front Left: Butter, covered, 7" long, **$95**; **Front Center**: Shaker, 3.25" tall, **$40**;
Front Right: Marmalades, covered, 5.75" tall on oval 8.5" long tray, **$350**

Original American Crystal label, 1917
Note: This label is very rarely found

Crystal, #2352, juice tumbler, 2.6"
tall, 1917 to 1937, **$30**
This tumbler was found with the
original American Crystal label, which
represents most of the value in this
case.

Left:
Crystal, Botanical
#1612, Ashtray, 5"
wide, sculptured floral,
1928 to 1930, **$100**
Note: Came from Gus
Heisey auction

Below:
Crystal, Kalonyal
#1776, Covered Butter,
6" tall, 8" wide, 1906 to
1909, **$250**

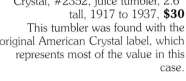

Crystal, Gascony #3397, Bowl, 10" wide, Krall floral cutting, 1932 to 1938, **$395**

Crystal, Gascony #3397, Sportsman Silhouette etching #455, Designed by Carl Cobel, 1932 to 1938
Left: Tumbler, 3" tall, 2.5 oz. **$60**; **Right**: Decanter, 11" tall, 16 ounce, **$275**

Crystal, Ball #4045, Vase, 6.5" tall, Wide optic, Mermaids etching #469, Designed by Carl Cobel, 1936 to 1953, **$450**

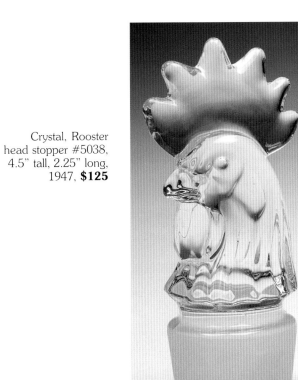

Crystal, National #4052, Shot Glass, 2" tall, 1.5 ounce, Tally Ho Silhouette etching #467, front view, 1933 to 1952, **$45**

Crystal, National #4052, Shot Glass, 2" tall, 1.5 ounce, Tally Ho Silhouette etching #467, back view, 1933 to 1952, **$45**

Crystal, Rooster head stopper #5038, 4.5" tall, 2.25" long, 1947, **$125**

Crystal, Coronation #4054, 1935 to 1957
Top: Soda Tumblers, 6.25" tall, **$18**; 4.75" tall, **$16**
Left to Right: Martini Pitcher, 8.5" tall, **$65**; Bar tumbler, 2.3" tall, **$18**; Soda Tumbler, 3.8" tall, **$15**; Bar Tumbler, 2" tall, **$24**; Pitcher, 10" tall, 1/2 gallon, **$125**

Original Heisey brochure advertising the Moonglo cutting

Crystal, Moonglo cutting #980
Left: National #4052, Tumbler, 5.25" tall, 10 ounce, 1942 to 1957, **$35**; **Right**: Gallagher #4164, Pitcher, 8" tall, 73 ounce, 1942 to 1957, **$250**

DAWN

Although *Dawn* was introduced in 1955, experimentation to achieve this color began in 1952. Notes were given on different formulas to indicate who assisted Olson with what formula and what name was given. In October of 1952, *Lead Smoke* was assisted by C. Reed and *Lime Smoke* was assisted by R. R. Shively. In 1953, there were three more color variations of this charcoal color. In January, there was *Green Smoke* by Pop Frasier. In February, there were two more formulas, plain *Smoke* and *Gill Lead* by R. R. Shively. The *Dawn* name first appears with another formula with R. R. Shively on February 26, 1953. More entries were made in July of 1954 and January of 1955, with changes to the formula.

Dawn was the last new color Heisey produced before it was closed in December of 1957 and was advertised as a transparent smoke or charcoal color. In a let-ter to Olson from R. R. Shively, Vice President of Drakenfeld & Co., on January 2, 1953, Shively explained the smoked glass formula he was sending and how to adapt it to make a darker color. A note scratched by the formula in Olson's notebook states *Swedish Smoke Glass*, and one would assume that was the color he was trying to obtain. When sunlight reflects on this color, you can see a hint of amethyst. In the marketing promotion for *Dawn*, the color was listed as a very versatile imitation of charcoal. Some of the patterns that can be found in *Dawn* are: Cabochon, Lodestar, and Roundelay. This color can, as in the case of the Lodestar single candle holder, be so intense that it looks almost black.

Duncan first produced a similar color they called *Teakwood*, and later they produced a lighter version they called *Smoke*. When Fostoria and Tiffin produced a similar color, they called it *Smoke*.

Dawn, Octagon #500, Handled Relish tray, 4 part, 9" wide, 14" long, 1955 to 1957, **$325**

Dawn, 20th Century #1415, 1956 to 1957 **Left**: Sundae, 2.5" tall, **$36**; **Center**: Juice, 4" tall, **$45**; **Right**: Soda, 5.8" tall, **$65**

Dawn, 20th Century #1415, Juice Pitcher, 5" tall, 18 ounce, 1956 to 1957, **$85**

Dawn, Saturn #1485, Vase, 10.5" tall, 1955 to 1957, **$395**

Dawn, Saturn #1485, 1955 to 1957
Left & Right: Shaker, 3.25" tall, **$98 each**; **Center**: Cruet, 6.75" tall, **$325**

Dawn, Crystolite #1503, Bowl, 10.5" wide, 1955 to 1957, **$250**

Dawn, Lodestar #1632,
Ashtray, 2" tall, 5.25" wide,
1955 to 1957, **$125**

Dawn, Lodestar #1632, 1955 to 1957
Left: Candle bowl, 2.25" tall, 4.25" wide,
$98; **Center**: Relish, 10.25", **$110** ;
Right: Pitcher, 8" tall, **$225**

Dawn, Lodestar #1632, 1955 to 1957
Left: Duo candlestick, 5.5" tall, 8" wide, **$195**; **Right**: Star candle
block, 2.5" tall, 5" wide, **$125**

Dawn, Lodestar #1632,
Covered Candy, 5" tall, 5.5"
wide, 1955 to 1957, **$275**

Dawn, Lodestar #1632, 1955 to 1957
Left: Creamer, no handle version, 2.75"
tall, **$65**; **Right**: Creamer, handled,
2.75" tall, **$50**

Dawn, Lodestar #1632, Relish, 7.5" wide, three part, 1955 to 1957, **$175**

Dawn, Glenford #3481, Swirl Optic, Tumbler, Blown, footed, 4" tall, 1953, **Market price undetermined**
This color is slightly different and is assumed to be from an early trial of the Smoke formula from R. R. Shively in February 1953.

Dawn, Town and Country #1637, Mayonnaise bowl, 5.25" wide, plate, 7.5" wide, 1955 to 1957, **$75 set**

Dawn, Screen Optic, Tumbler, Blown, 4.5" tall, 1955, **Market price undetermined**
Experimental pattern; Presumably to be Heisey since it came from Louise Reame's house. Only two are known to exist.

Original Heisey brochure
advertising Cabochon

Dawn, Cabochon #1951,
Covered candy, flat, 4" tall,
6.5" wide, 1955, **$350**

Below:
Dawn, Cabochon #1951, 1955
Left: .25 pound covered butter,
2.5" tall, 7" long, **$195**; **Right**:
Creamer, 3.75" tall, **$85**

EMERALD

Emerald was one of the first colors Heisey produced. It was introduced about 1896 and on pieces from the early years is frequently found with a gold rim decoration. The color is a dark green transparent that is very rich looking. The color was discontinued in 1902.

Every major glass company produced their version of an emerald green color. Cambridge, Fenton, Fostoria, New Martinsville, Northwood, and U.S. Glass Company also called their dark green color *Emerald*. The late Victorian pattern glass made by U.S. Glass Company most resemble Heisey's color.

Emerald, Fancy Loop #1205, Punch cup, 2.25" tall, 1896 to 1909, **$35**

Emerald, Pointed Oval in Diamond Point #150, Butter bottom, 5.5" wide, 1898 to 1903, **$40**

Emerald, Fancy Loop #1205, 1896 to 1909
Left: Sugar, 2" tall, **$40**; **Right**: Creamer, 2.25" tall, **$45**

Emerald, Pointed Oval in Diamond Point #150, 1898 to 1903
Left: Spooner, 3.25" tall, **$65**; **Center**: Covered Sugar, 4.75" tall, **$95**; **Right**: Creamer, 3.5" tall, **$45**

Emerald, Fancy Loop #1205, Tumbler, 3.8" tall, gold accents, 1896 to 1909, **$70**

Emerald, Star and Zipper #1245, Bowl, 9" wide, 1897 to 1903, **$175**

Emerald, Pineapple and Fan #1255, Covered Butter, 5" tall, 7.5" wide, 1898 to 1907, **$225**

Emerald Green, Gold accents, toothpicks
Top: Fancy Loop #1205, 2.5" tall, 1896 to 1909, **$70**
Bottom Left: Winged Scroll #1280, 2.25" tall, 1899 to 1901, **$68**;
Bottom Right: Pineapple and Fan #1255, 2.25" tall, 1898 to 1907, **$65**

Emerald, Pineapple Fan #1255, Punch cup, 2" tall, 1898 to 1907, **$60**

Emerald, Pineapple and Fan #1255, Sugar, 2.75" tall, 1898 to 1907, **$50**

Emerald, Pineapple and Fan #1255, Spooner, 4" tall, 1898 to 1907, **$95**

Emerald, Pineapple and Fan #1255, 1898 to 1907
Left: Covered Sugar, 6.25" tall, **$90**; **Right**: Creamer, 4.25" tall, **$70**

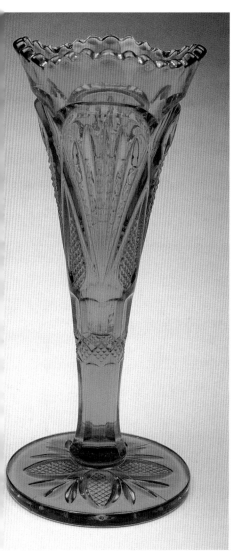

Left:
Emerald Green, Pineapple and Fan #1255,
Vase, footed, 6.25" tall, 1898 to 1907, **$125**

Emerald Green, Winged Scroll #1280, bowl, 8.75" wide, 1899 to 1901, **$295**

Emerald, Winged Scroll #1280, 1899 to 1901
Top: Ash Receiver, 1.6" tall, **$195**
Bottom Row: Left: Match holder, 2.25" tall, **$350** (not to be
confused with the toothpick); **Center**: Cigarette holder, 2.75" tall,
$245; **Right**: Humidor, missing lid, 4" tall, **$175**

Emerald, Winged Scroll #1280, Covered Butter, 4.5" tall, 7.5" wide, 1899 to 1901, **$145**

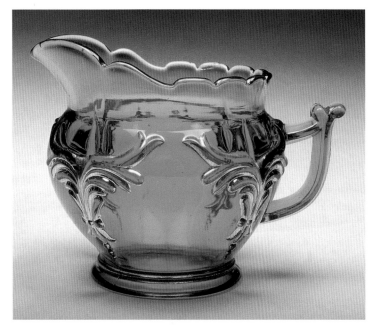

Emerald, Winged Scroll #1280, Creamer, 4.25" tall, 1899 to 1901, **$60**

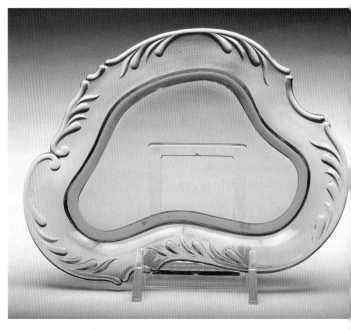

Emerald, Winged Scroll #1280, Pin Tray, 5.5" long, 1899 to 1901, **$125**

Emerald, Winged Scroll #1280, Spooner, 3.5" tall, 1899 to 1901, **$75**

Emerald, Beaded Swag #1295, 1897 to 1913
Left: Spooner, 4" tall, **$75**; **Right**: Creamer, 4.5" tall, **$50**

FLAMINGO

Flamingo was introduced in 1925 and was made until 1935. This is a transparent pink color that can range from pale to a darker rose. There tends to be an orange tint in this color. The various levels of the chemicals Sodium Arsenate, Sodium Selenite, and Metallic Selenium influence the tints of this color. The flamingo bird was the inspiration for the name. A special paper label was developed for it with the flamingo bird shown. This was probably one of the best-designed labels of all, with the play on words thrown in for good measure. From the time it was introduced, *Flamingo* was sought after. As a result, a great many items were produced in this color. Full sets of Empress, Pleat & Panel, Twist, and Yeoman patterns can be assembled in this color.

Original Flamingo label

Moongleam was a companion color of green to go with the pink *Flamingo* color. The idea was to make pink and green items that were selling well for the other glass companies of their time period. Many collectors and dealers refer to these colors as Depression Era. Most of the glass companies produced a version of pink or rose. Fenton and Fostoria both called their pink *Rose.*

Flamingo, Jack-Be-Nimble #31, Toy Candlestick, 2" tall, 1925 to 1935, **$250**

Flamingo, Lil Squatter #99, Candle holder, 1.5" tall, 3.75" wide, 1925 to 1935, **$25**

Flamingo, Oakleaf #10, coaster, 4" wide, 1925, **$20**

Flamingo, Wellington #107, Candlestick, 10.25" tall, 1925 to 1930, **$250**

Flamingo, Petticoat Dolphin
#109, 1925 to 1935
Left and Right: Candlestick,
5.75" tall, **$195 each**; **Center**:
Comport, 7.25" tall, 7.75"
wide, **$235**

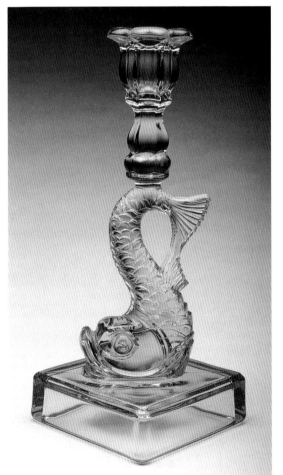

Right:
Flamingo, Dolphin #110,
Candlestick, 10.75" tall, 1925
to 1935, **$250**

Far right:
Flamingo, Cherub #111,
Candlestick, 11.25" tall, 1926
to 1929, **$500**

Flamingo, Mercury #112, Candlesticks, 3.75" tall, 4.75" wide, 1926 to 1930, **$75 pair**

Flamingo, Charter Oak #116, Candlestick, 3" tall, 1926 to 1929, **$75**

Flamingo, Tricorn #129, three light candlestick, 5" tall, 1929 to 1935, **$145**

Flamingo, Acorn #130, Candlestick, 4" tall, 5.5" long, 1929, **$395**

Flamingo, Triplex #136, three light candlestick, 6.4" tall, 6.75" long, 1931 to 1935, **$195**

Flamingo, Wide Flat Panel #354, Stacking Butter pat, Sugar and Creamer, 3.5" tall, 1905 to 1935, **$165**

Flamingo, Wide Flat Panel #354, 1905 to 1935
Left: Sugar, 4.25" tall, **$85**; **Right**: Creamer, 4.25" tall, **$75**

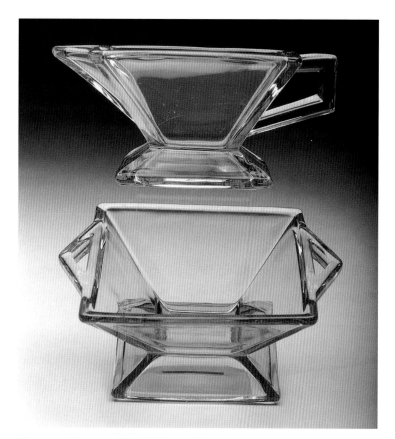

Flamingo, Quator #355, 1913 to 1935
Bottom: Sugar, 2.4" tall, **$95**; **Top**: Creamer, 2.5" tall, **$85**

Flamingo, Tudor #411, Cigarette jar, 5" tall, 1923 to 1939, **$165**

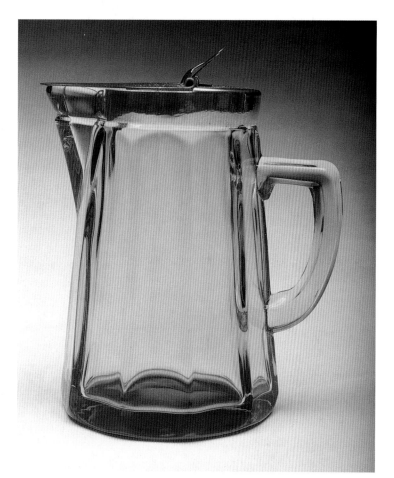

Flamingo, McGrady #372, Syrup, 5" tall, 1929 to 1948, **$135**

Flamingo, Double Rib and Panel #417, Covered mustard jar, 1923 to 1939, **$110**

Flamingo, Tudor #414,
Covered Hotel Sugar, 5" tall,
1923 to 1939, **$150**

Flamingo, Grecian Border
(Greek Key) #433, 1925 to
1929
Left: Punch bowl and base,
bowl, 7.5" tall, 14.5" wide;
base, 7.75" tall, 9.5" wide,
$2750; **Right**: punch cup,
2.15" tall, **$85**

Flamingo, Picket #458, Basket, 9" tall, 7.25" wide, 1933 to 1935, **$350**

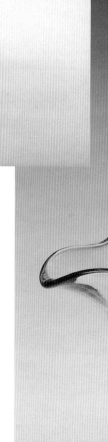

Flamingo, Bonnet #463, Basket, 13.25" tall, 7.75" long, 1925 to 1933, **$425**

Flamingo, Helmet #467
Basket, 10.25" tall, 10.5" long,
oval, 1925 to 1933, **$700**

Original advertising, Glass Secrets series, "A Crystal Bubble Amazed
the World", from Good Housekeeping September 1928, featured
Flamingo color

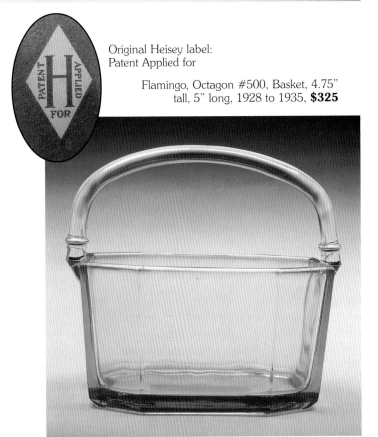

Original Heisey label:
Patent Applied for

Flamingo, Octagon #500, Basket, 4.75"
tall, 5" long, 1928 to 1935, **$325**

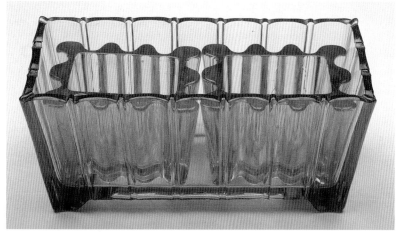

Flamingo, Fogg #501, Window box with two flower frog inserts, 3.8" tall, 8" long, 3" wide, 1929 to 1933, **$275**

Flamingo, Colognes
Left: Circle #517, 6" tall, .25 ounce, 1925 to 1933, **$225**; **Center**: Fairacre #516, 5" tall, 1 ounce, 1925 to 1933, **$245**; **Right**: Taper #515, 6.25" tall, .25 ounce, 1925 to 1933, **$225**

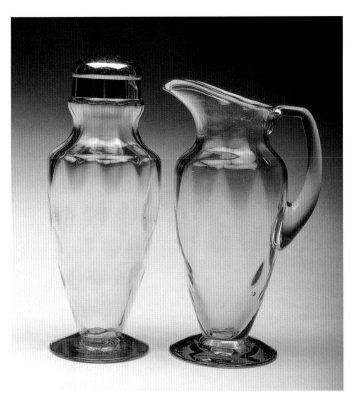

Flamingo, Caswell #1001, 1925 to 1933
Left: Sugar Shaker, 6" tall, **$95**; **Right**: Creamer, 5.5" tall, **$65**

Flamingo, Pleat and Panel #1170, Covered Candy, 6.2" tall, footed, short stem (listed as comport) 6" wide, 1925 to 1935, **$75**

Flamingo, Pleat and Panel #1170, 1925 to 1935
Top Row: Left: Plate, 8" wide, lunch, **$15**; **Right**: Plate, 10.6" wide, dinner, **$40**
Bottom Row: Left: Bowl, 4.4" wide, Chow Chow, **$18**; **Center**: Creamer, 2.6" tall, **$32**; **Right**: Cup and saucer, coffee, **$45**

Flamingo, Pleat and Panel #1170, 1925 to 1935
Left: Vase, hat shape, 3.6" tall, **$125**; **Right**: Cruet, 4.75" tall,
$110

Flamingo, Revere #1183 French Dressing Boat, 3.4" tall, 6.8" long,
Liner, 6.75" long, 5.75" wide, 1925 to 1935, **$135**
Note: This set has the original Flamingo label still on it.

Flamingo, *Revere* #1183, Salt dip, 1.85" wide, 1925 to 1935, **$45**

Flamingo, Yeoman #1184, Mustard Jar with spoon, 3.5" tall, 1925 to 1935, **$275**

Left:
Flamingo, Yeoman #1184, Punch Cup, 2" tall, 1925 to 1935, **$30**

Flamingo, Yeoman #1184, Covered Candy, 4" tall, 6" wide, 1925 to 1935, **$85**

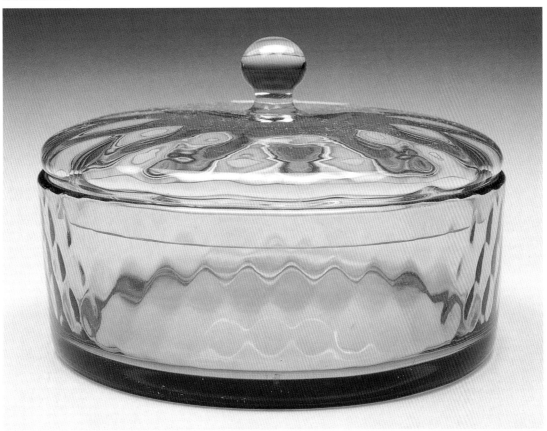

Flamingo, Yeoman #1184, Smoking set- seven piece, handled tray, 4.5" tall, 7" long, 6 ashtrays, 3" long, 3" wide, 1925 to 1935, **$245**

Flamingo, Yeoman #1184, 1925 to 1935
Top Row: Diamond Optic, Sugar, 3.5" tall, **$45**; Creamer, 3" tall, **$40**
Bottom Row: Plain, Sugar, 3.5" tall, **$40**; Creamer, 3" tall, **$35**

Flamingo, Yeoman #1189, Individual, 1925 to 1935
Left: Covered Sugar, 3.75" tall, **$100**; **Right**: Creamer, 2.75" tall, **$85**

Flamingo, Twist #1252, 1928 to 1935
Top Row: Left: Bowl, 9.25" wide, **$75**; **Right**: Bowl, 12.25" wide, **$98**
Bottom Row: Left: Bowl, jelly, 6" wide, **$35**; Cruet: 4.75" tall, **$145**; **Right**: Bowl, 12.5" wide, **$125**

Flamingo, Beehive #1238, plate, 8" wide, 1925 to 1935, **$30**

Flamingo, Twist #1252, 1928 to 1935
Left: Mustard, 4" tall, **$95**; **Right**: Cruet, 4.75" tall, **$145**

Flamingo, Twist #1252, Covered Mustard with #5 spoon and under plate, 3.75" tall, 4.25" wide, 1928 to 1935, **$250**

Flamingo, Twist #1252, Footed Almond or Individual Sugar, 2.5" tall, 1928 to 1935, **$58**

Flamingo, Empress #1401, round foot, 1930 to 1935 **Left**: Creamer, 3" tall, **$45**; **Right**: Sugar, 3" tall, **$50**

Flamingo, Empress #1401, 1930
to 1935
Left: Mustard, 3.5" tall, **$145**;
Right: Cruet, 6.25" tall, **$165**

Flamingo, Empress #1401, Punch cup,
2.25" tall, 1930 to 1935, **$40**

Flamingo, Half Circle #1403, 1930 to 1935
Left: Sugar, 2.75" tall, **$60**; **Right**: Creamer, 2.75" tall, **$55**

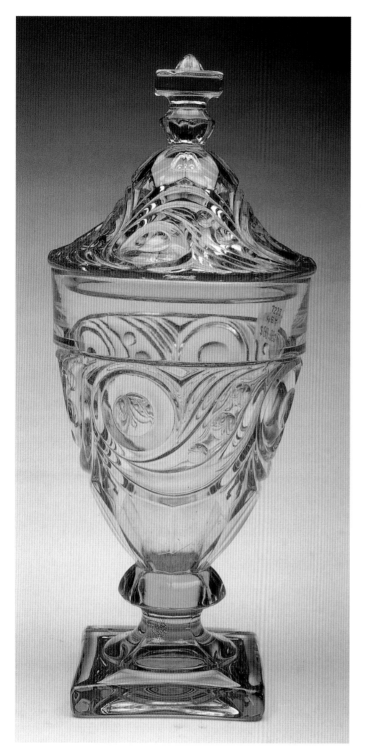

Flamingo, Ipswich #1405, Covered
Candy, 8.5" tall, 3.5" wide, 1931 to
1935, **$800**

Flamingo, Warwick #1428,
Horn of Plenty Vase, 9" tall,
7.5" long, 1933 to 1935, **$650**

Flamingo, Aristocrat
#1430, Covered
Candy, 10.75" tall,
1933 to 1935, **$1200**

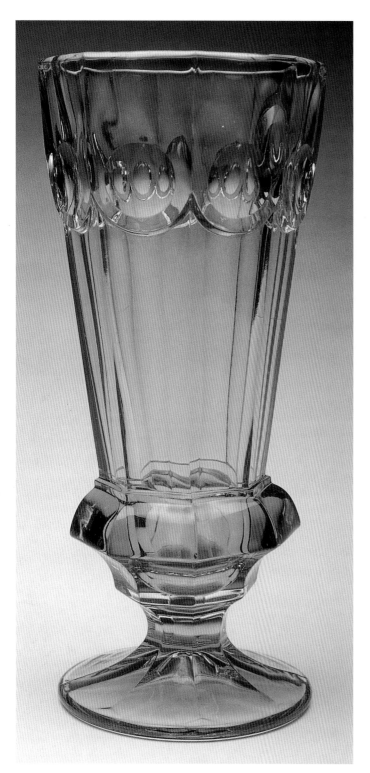

Flamingo, Thumbprint and Panel #1433, Vase, 8.5" tall, 1934 to 1935, **$195**

Flamingo, Jamestown #3408, Beer Mug, 4" tall, 1933 to 1935, **$175**

Original advertising, Famous Inns and Hotels series, Long Island Duckling Bigarade, House Beautiful September 1926, featuring Flamingo color

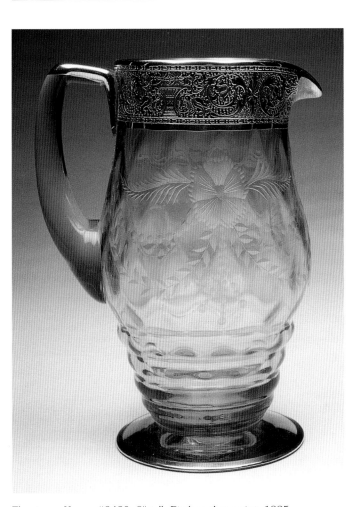

Flamingo, Koors #3480, 9" tall, Pitcher, three pint, 1925
to 1937, **$145**

Flamingo, Elaine #4214, Vase, Swirl Optic, 7.5" tall, 1925, **$85**

Flamingo, Colognes
Left: #4035, Duck perfume bottle, 4.5" tall, .75 ounce,
1929 to 1933, **$245**; **Right**: Seven Circle #4034, 4.5"
tall, .75 ounce, 1929 to 1933, **$225**

Flamingo, Frances #4217, Vase, Diamond Optic, 6" tall, 1925 to 1937, **$85**

Flamingo, Mike Owens bust, 5" tall, 5" wide, marked on front: 1859 M. J. Owens 1923 (Made for Edward Libbey of Libbey Owens Glass Company. Mike Owens designed the machinery for automated glass production and this piece was to honor his achievements.), 1925, **$750**

Flamingo, Diamond Optic, favor vases, 1933 to 1935
Left to right: #4227, 3" tall, **$475**; #4228, 3" tall, **$410**; #4229, 3" tall, **$600**; #4230, 3", **$1000**; #4231, 3" tall, **$550**; #4232, 3" tall, **$480**

HAWTHORNE

Hawthorne is a transparent, light amethyst color that has a brownish tinge. The color was developed in 1926 and introduced in 1927. At the bottom of the *Flamingo* color formula in Olson's notebook was a note he wrote that said, "add 4 6/10 oz. of Powdered Blue to this formula to make the color of Hawthorn." This is the only mention of this color in his notebook.

Hawthorne was made for a relatively short time. The public was not responsive to this color, since it had a muddy appearance, and lacked the brilliance of other Heisey colors. After many attempts were made to generate sales, the color was discontinued by the end of 1927. Some people have tried to pass off pieces of sun colored glassware as *Hawthorne*. You should notice the color closely, so you do not mistake a sun-colored piece.

Original Hawthorne label

Hawthorne, Pinwheel #121, Candlesticks, 2" tall, 4.5" wide, 1927, **$125 pair**

Hawthorne, #15, Flower frog with Mercury #123, Candlestick, 6" tall, 5.25" wide, two piece, 1927, **$275**

Hawthorne, Medium Flat Panel #353, Individual Almond, 1.75" tall, 2.75" wide, 1927, **$35**

Hawthorne, Coarse Rib #406, 1927
Left: Creamer, 3.25" tall, **$60**; **Right**: Covered Sugar, 4.5" tall, **$85**

Hawthorne, Tudor #411, Covered Candy, 5.5" tall, 5.5" wide, footed, 1927, **$125**

Hawthorne, Tudor #411, Mayonnaise Bowl, 4.5" wide, plate 5.6" wide, Ladle, 1927, **$265**

Hawthorne, Tudor #411, 1927
Left; Sugar, 3" tall, **$40**;
Right: Creamer, 3" tall, **$35**

Hawthorne, Tudor #414, Covered Hotel
Sugar, 5" tall, 1927, **$175**

Advertising
of a Heisey
basket from
National
Geographic
April 1925

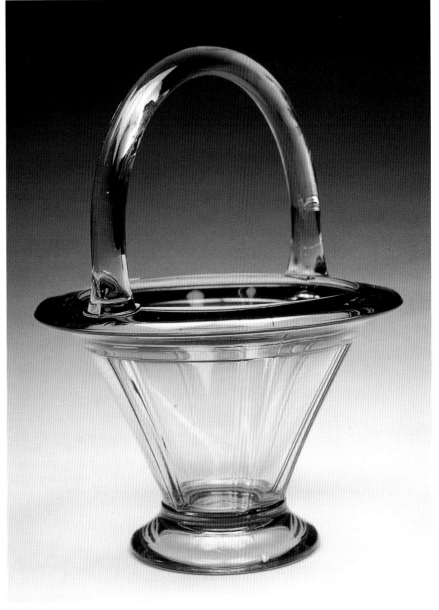

Hawthorne, Double Rib and Panel #417, Basket, 8" tall, 6.25" wide, 1927,
$350

Hawthorne, Petal #479, 1927
Left: Hotel Sugar, 4" tall, **$95**; **Right**: Hotel Creamer, 4.25" tall, **$75**

Hawthorne, Taper #515, Cologne,
6.25" tall, Diamond Optic, 1927, **$250**

Hawthorne, Caswell #1001, Sugar
Shaker, 6" tall, Diamond Optic, 1927,
$100

Hawthorne, Yeoman #1184, 1927
Back: Plate, 8" wide, **$30**; Tumbler, 4.25" tall, **$48**
Left: Crystal Store display sign; Comport, 4" tall, 6.5" wide, **$72**; **Center**: Cup, 2" tall and Saucer, 6.25" wide, **$55**; **Right**: Sherbet, 2.75" tall, **$20**

Hawthorne, Yeoman #1184, Tumbler, juice, 4" tall, 1927, **$40**

Hawthorne, Yeoman #1184, 1927
Left: Tumbler, 4.25" tall, **$72**; **Right**: Pitcher, 7.75" tall, **$475**

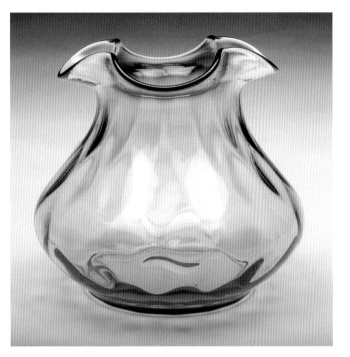

Hawthorne, Yeoman #1184, Vase, 6.5" tall, 1927, **$150**

Hawthorne, Octagon #1229, Individual nut cup, 1" tall, 4.25" wide, 1927, **$30**

Hawthorne, Koors #3480, Pitcher, 9" tall, three pint, Rib Optic, 1927, **$285**

Hawthorne, Steele #4157, Rose Bowl, 5.75" tall, Diamond Optic, 1927, **$198**

IVORINA VERDE AND IVORY

Introduced in 1897, *Ivorina Verde* was Heisey's version of custard glass. It was an opaque, dark creamy yellow glass. A lighter version of this color is called *Ivory*. Both versions of this color fluoresce under a black light. In the early years, many of the pieces made were used as souvenir items with advertising on them. This color was only made for a short time; our best estimate is that this color ended about 1904. Heisey's sales people must have pushed to get this color to compete with Northwood's *Custard*, that was selling well during the time period.

Ivorina Verde, Ringed Band #310, Punch cup, 2.35" tall, 1900, **$25**

Ivorina Verde, Cane and Bar #8047, Creamer, 4.75" tall, Minneapolis, Kansas, floral decoration, 1900, **$65**

Ivorina Verde, Ringed Band #310, Covered Butter, 5.75" tall, 7.25" wide, 1900, **$145**

Left:
Ivorina Verde, Ringed Band #310, 1900
Top: Toothpick 2.25" tall, **$60**
Bottom Left: Spooner, 4.25" tall, **$85**; **Bottom Center**: Covered Sugar, 6.5" tall, **$75**; **Bottom Right**: Creamer, 4.75" tall, **$55**

Ivorina Verde, Souvenir cups
Top: Stitch #1101, 2" tall, Presho, SD, floral decoration, 1897, **$25**
Bottom: Left: Stitch #1101, 2" tall, Pittston, PA, 1897, **$25**; **Bottom Right**: Ringed Band #310, 2.25" tall, Wishek, ND, 1900, **$35**

Ivorina Verde, Stitch #1101, Punch cup, 2" tall, Floral decoration, Souvenir Eldred, Minn., 1897, **$35**

Below:
Ivorina Verde, Cut Block #1200, Creamer, 3.25" tall, souvenir advertising, 1896 to 1899
Top Row: Houtzdale, PA, **$40**; Calumet, Mich., **$40**
Bottom Row: Meridian, Wis., **$48**; Blackwell, Okla, **$48**.; Eureka, Kans., **$48**

Ivorina Verde, Cut Block #1200, sugar, 2.5" tall, souvenir advertising, 1896 to 1899, **$40 each**
Top: Vandling, Pa.; Larned, Kans.; **Bottom**: Merricourt, N.D.; Ottawa, Kans.; Arkansas City, Kans.

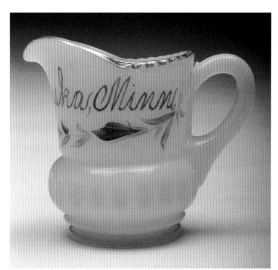

Ivorina Verde, Cut Block #1200, advertising Medford, Ore., 1896 to 1899
Left: Sugar, 2.5" tall, **$35**; **Right**: Creamer, 3.25" tall, **$40**

Ivorina Verde, Punty Band #1220, Creamer, 2.75" tall, souvenir advertising, Minneiska, Minn., 1897, **$45**

Ivorina Verde, Pineapple and Fan #1255, Creamer, 4.75" tall, Ellsworth, Kansas advertising, floral decoration, 1898 to 1907, **$60**

Ivorina Verde, Winged Scroll #1280, 1899 to 1901 **Left**: Creamer, 4" tall, **$55**; **Right**: Covered sugar, 5" tall, **$75**

Ivorina Verde, Winged Scroll #1280, Gold accents, 1899 to 1901
Left: Creamer, 4" tall, **$70**; **Right**: Covered Sugar, 5" tall, **$95**

Ivorina Verde, Winged Scroll #1280, Punch cup, 2" tall, 1899 to 1901, **$125**

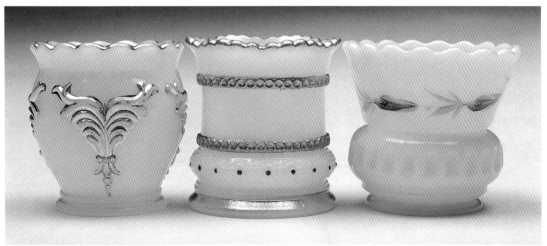

Ivorina Verde, toothpicks
Left: Winged Scroll #1280, 2.25" tall, 1899 to 1901, **$80**; **Center**: Ringed Band #310, 2.25" tall, 1900, **$65**;
Right: Punty Band #1220, 2.25" tall, 1897, **$48**

MARIGOLD

Marigold was Heisey's version of a dark yellow color and was introduced in 1927. The color takes on a yellow-orange tint and was named for the marigold flower. It was advertised as having a sparkling sheen. The bright golden color was achieved by adding uranium salts in the formula. Under a black light, this color will fluoresce to green. There were many problems with the formula that caused the glass to deteriorate and have a rough texture. The deterioration is sometimes referred to as a "sugared effect" by collectors. Several attempts were made to change the formula to correct the problem, but finally it was discontinued in 1928.

The U.S. Glass Company produced a color called *Old Gold* that was very similar to *Marigold*. Most, if not all, of their pieces were marked with their logo "USG."

Marigold, Liberty #128, Candlestick, 3.25" tall, 1928, **$125**

Marigold, Tricorn #129, Candlestick, three light, 5" tall, 6.5" wide, 1928, **$300**

Marigold, Quator #355, 1927 to 1928
Left: Sugar, 2.4" tall, **$100**; **Right**: Creamer, 2.5" Tall, **$100**

Marigold, detail of sugared effect

Marigold, Octagon #500, Basket, 4.5"
tall, 5.5" long, 1927 to 1928, **$850**

Marigold, Octagon #500,
Creamer, 2.5" tall, 1928, **$75**

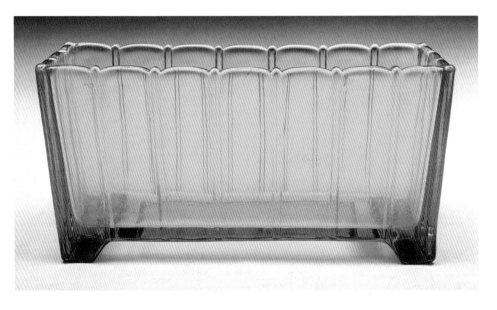

Marigold, Fogg #501, Window
box, 4" tall, 8" long, 3" wide,
1927 to 1928, **$195**

Marigold, Yeoman #1184, Covered Candy box, 4" tall, 6" wide, 1927 to 1928, **$175**

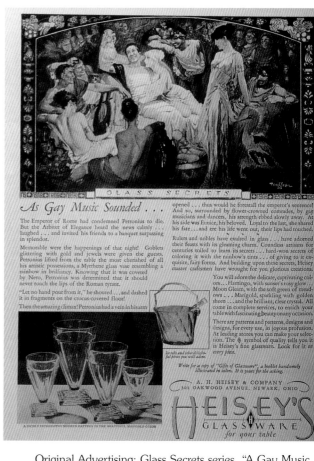

Original Advertising: Glass Secrets series, "A Gay Music Sounded", from Good Housekeeping May 1929, featured Marigold color

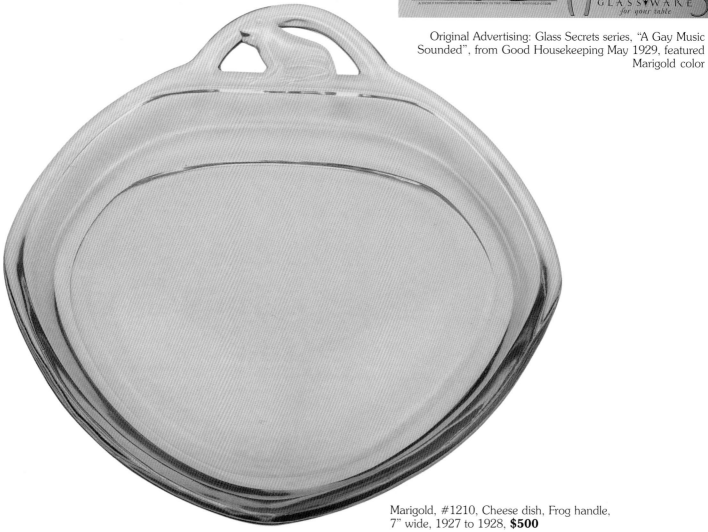

Marigold, #1210, Cheese dish, Frog handle, 7" wide, 1927 to 1928, **$500**

Marigold, Twist #1252, Covered Candy, three corner mint, 3.75" tall, 6.5" wide, 1927 to 1928, **$145**

Marigold Twist #1252, 1927 to 1928
Left: Plate, 4.5" wide, **$35**; **Right**: Octagon #500, Custard, 2" tall, 2.75" long, 4 tab feet, **$95**

Marigold, Twist #1252, 1927 to 1928
Back: Platter, 15.25" long, **$125**
Front Center: Footed Almond, 3" tall, **$55**; Cream Soup, 5" wide, **$100**
Front: Leaf relish, 7" long, **$50**; Sugar, 3.5" tall, **$45**; **Right**: Cruet, 5" tall, **$225**

Marigold, Twist #1252, Hotel, oval, 1927 to 1928
Left: Sugar, 3.25" tall, **$80**; **Right**: Creamer, 4.25" tall, **$80**

MOONGLEAM

Moongleam was a revision of the original *Emerald* green formula. It was lightened to produce a new pastel color that was introduced in 1925. This color was advertised in women's magazines under the heading "The Green of Moonlight on the Sea." Production ended about 1935. *Moongleam* was the third most popular color at Heisey. It is another Heisey color that will vary from light to dark and some pieces even tend to take on a little blue tint. Other pieces can run so dark to remind you of *Emerald*. This color competed with other glass houses making green glassware. A pastel green was produced at all the major glass companies.

Original Heisey brochure advertising Moongleam

Left:
Moongleam, Old Williamsburg #2, Candlestick, 7.75" tall, 1925 to 1935, **$1000**

Moongleam, Patrician #5, Candelabra with prisms, 12" tall, 1925 to 1931, **$500**

Moongleam, Jack Be Nimble #31, Toy Candlestick, 2" tall, 1925 to 1935, **$150**

Moongleam, Bertha #104, Candlestick, 5.5" tall, 1925 to 1929, **$800**

Moongleam, Pembroke #105, Candelabra, 1925 to 1934
Left: 9.5" tall, floral cutting, not Heisey decorating, **$250**;
Right: 6.5" tall, **$150**

Moongleam, Wellington #107, Candlestick, 10.5" tall, 1925 to 1930, **$350**

Moongleam, Petticoat Dolphin #109, 1925 to 1935
Left and Right: Candlestick, 6.5" tall, **$225 each**; **Center**; Comport, 8" tall, 7.5" wide, **$245**

Moongleam, Cherub #111, Candlestick, 11.5" tall, satin finish, 1926 to 1929, **$750**

Moongleam, Mercury #112, Candlesticks, 1926 to 1935
Left: 3.75" tall, **$45**;
Center: 8.75" tall, **$200**;
Right: 5.5" tall, flower frog combination #123, **$175**

Left:
Moongleam, Bamboo #117, Candlestick, 7.5" tall, 1927 to 1929, **$1000 each**
Left: Moongleam candle cup; **Right**: Moongleam stem and base

Moongleam, Overlapping Swirl #120, Candlestick, 3" tall, 1927 to 1931, **$45**

Moongleam, Twist Stem #127, Candlestick, 4.75" tall, 1929, **$750**

Moongleam, Tricorn #129, candle holders, 5" tall, 1929 to 1935
Left: Moongleam base, **$175**; **Right**: Solid color, **$150**

Moongleam, Triplex #136, Candlestick, three light, 6.5" tall, 7" long, 1931 to 1935, **$250**

Moongleam, Concave Circle #137, Candlestick, 5" tall, 1931 to 1933, **$750**

Moongleam, Banded Flute #150, Tray, 13.25" wide, 1925 to 1932, **$225**

Moongleam, Pinwheel and Fan #350, Punch Cup
2.25" tall, 1925, **$35**

Moongleam, Flat Panel #352, Tobacco Humidor,
7" tall, 16 ounce, 1925 to 1929, **$650**

Moongleam, Quator #355, 1925 to 1935
Top: Creamer, 2.5" tall, **$40**; **Bottom**:
Sugar, 2.25" tall, **$40**

Moongleam, Irwin #361, Cigarette box/ Ashtray combination, 5.5" tall, 5.25" long, 1928 to 1935, **$195**

Moongleam, McGrady #372, Syrup, 3.75" tall, 1929 to 1935, **$145**

Moongleam, McGrady #372, Syrup, 5" tall, 1929 to 1935, **$195**

Moongleam, Narrow Flute #393, Individual, 1925 to 1935
Left: Sugar 2.25" tall, **$30**; **Right**: Creamer, 2.25" tall, **$30**

*T*he immense vogue of Heisey's Glassware in colors reveals a happy interpretation of people's desires. The delightful shades add a rich beauty to the table, their charming delicacy implies discriminating taste. As gifts, these creations win wonder and admiration.

Remembrances certain to please. No. 419 Jacobean Goblet, with crystal foot. No. 1183 Candy Box. No. 4191 Vase with crystal top and Moon Gleam foot. No. 367 Decanter with cut stopper of crystal

Below—Pieces of real utility. No. 411 design. In front—footed Preserve, Mint Dish (Moon Gleam and crystal). In back—Oyster Cocktail (crystal only), Sugar and Cream (with Moon Gleam handles).

[5]

Original Heisey booklet, "Gifts of Glassware", page 5 showing Moongleam, 1928

Moongleam, Tudor #411, Moongleam handles, 1925 to 1935
Left: Covered Sugar, 4.75" tall, **$75**; **Right**: Creamer, 3" tall, **$50**

Moongleam, Tudor #412, Cigarette box with ashtray top, 4" tall, 4.25" wide, 1925 to 1935, **$300** **Left**: Shown complete; **Center**: Bottom section; **Right**: Ashtray combination lid

Moongleam, Double Rib and Panel #417, Covered mustard jar, 3" tall, 1925 to 1935, **$125**

Left:
Moongleam, Double Rib and Panel #417, Basket, 6" wide, floral cutting, 1925 to 1935, **$275**

Moongleam, Grape Leaf Square #441, 4.75" wide, 1927 to 1933
Left: Satin finish, **$65**; **Right**: Plain gloss finish, **$100**
Note: This was Heisey's only attempt to imitate the sculptured glass that Lalique was making. It was marketed as a Lalique style.

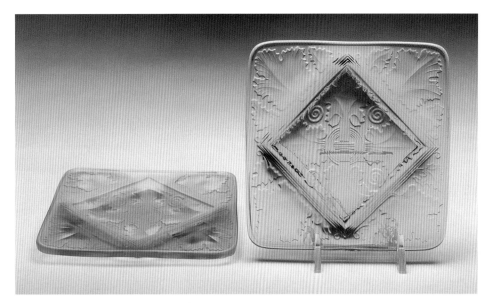

Moongleam, Bonnet #463, Basket, 13" tall, 8" long, 1925 to 1935, **$500**

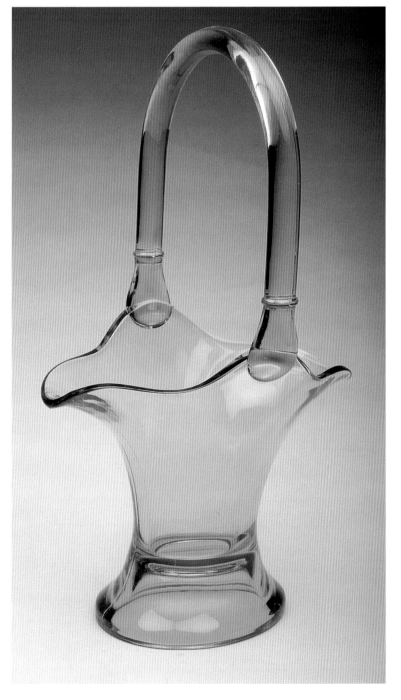

Moongleam, Recessed Panel #465, Covered Candy, 9" tall, 4" wide, .5 pound, 1925 to 1935, **$750**

Advertising "Something Entirely New for your Table" from April 1915

Moongleam, Cologne, Hexagon Stem #485, 6" tall, 1935, **$200**

Moongleam, Narrow Flute with Rim #473, Dice sugar tray, 5.25" wide, Creamer, 2.75" tall, 1925 to 1931, **$175 set**

Original advertising, Glass Secrets Series, "A Gift Esteemed Since Imperial Rome", from Good Housekeeping November 1928, features Moongleam color

Moongleam, Octagon #500, Basket, 4.5" tall, 5.5" long, 1928 to 1935, **$265**

Moongleam handles, Octagon #500, 1928 to 1935
Left: Creamer, 2.4" tall, **$35; Right**; Sugar, 2.5" tall, **$40**

Moongleam, Octagon #500, Creamer, 2.5" tall, 1928 to 1935, **$85**

Moongleam, Phyllis #1020, Sugar, 3.75 tall, marked in bottom: PAT 8/30/21, 1925 to 1933, **$60**

Moongleam, Colognes, Diamond Optic
Left: Fairacre #516, 5.25" tall, one ounce, 1925 to 1933, **$375**;
Right: Taper #515, 6.5" tall, .25 ounce, 1925 to 1933, **$295**

Moongleam, Pleat and Panel #1170, Covered Candy, 8.5" tall, 5.25" wide, 1925 to 1935, **$95**

Moongleam, Pleat and Panel #1170, Relish, 5 part, 10.5" wide, 1925 to 1935, **$85**

Below:
Moongleam, Yeoman #1184, handled bon bon, 1925 to 1935
Left: 8.5" long, 6.25" wide, **$45**; **Back Right**: 5.75" long, 4" wide, **$38**; **Front Right**: 4" long, 2.5" wide, **$35**

Original Heisey booklet, "Gifts of Glassware", page 32, Heisey's Glassware for your Table, showing Diamond Optic pitcher with Moongleam handle and foot

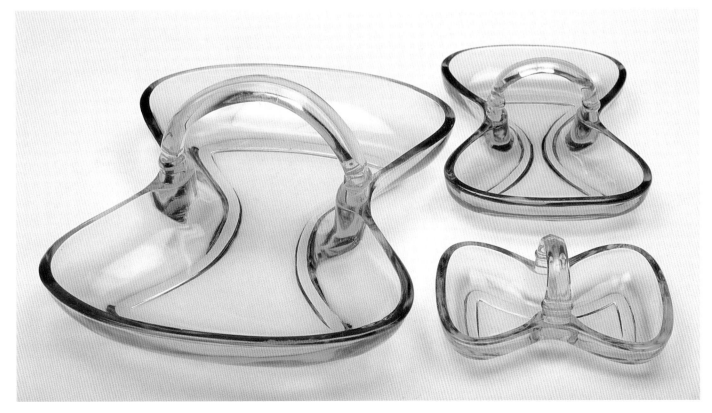

Moongleam, Yeoman #1184, 1925 to 1935
Left: Covered sugar, 3.5" tall, **$95**; **Right**: Creamer, 3" tall, **$70**

Below:
Moongleam, #1210, Cheese dish, frog handle, 7" wide, 1929 to 1933, **$135**

Moongleam, Twist #1252, 1928 to 1935, **$100 set**
Left: Candlestick, 2" tall, shown in different positions; **Right**: Bowl, 7.75"
wide

Original advertising, Glass Secrets Series, "In a Glasse a
Yard Long", from Good Housekeeping March 1929,
features Moongleam Twist

Below:
Moongleam, Twist #1252, 1928 to 1935
Left: Creamer, 4.5" tall, **$65**; **Right**: Sugar, 4.25" tall,
Silver overlay decoration, **$75**

Moongleam, Twist #1252, flat, Oval Hotel, 1928 to 1935
Left: Sugar, 3.25" tall, **$100**; **Right**: Creamer, 4.25", **$100**

Moongleam, Twist #1252, 1928 to 1935
Back Left: Creamer, 4.25" tall, 9 oz. **$75**; **Center**: Goblet, 7" tall, 10 ounce, **$65**
Front Left: Relish, 7" long, Oblong, **$30**; **Right**: Cup and Saucer, cup, 2.5" tall, 7 ounce; saucer, 5.8" wide, **$25**

Below:
Moongleam, Twist #1252, 1928 to 1935
Back Left: Plate, 8.25" wide, rectangular indent in center, Kraft Cheese, **$65**; **Back Right**: plate, 10.75" wide, dinner, **$160**; **Front Left**: Bowl, 9.25" wide, rolled edge, **$65**; **Front Right**: Ice bucket, 5.4" tall, 8.75" long, chrome handle, **$95**

Moongleam, Empress #1401, Lion Head Bowl, 10.75" wide, 1930 to 1935, **$600**

Moongleam, Empress #1401, 1930 to
1935, **$125 set**
Left: Sugar, 3" tall; **Right**: Creamer, 3.25"
tall
Bottom: Tray, 6" wide, 11" long, **$95**

Moongleam, Empress #1401, Dolphin
footed, 1930 to 1935
Left: Comport, 5.75" tall, 5.75" wide,
$225; **Right**: Candlestick, 6" tall, **$200**

Moongleam, Old Sandwich #1404, 1931 to 1935 **Left and Right**: Candlestick, 6.5" tall, **$125 each**; **Center**: Console Bowl, 4.5" tall, 12" long, **$125**

Moongleam, Ipswich #1405, Water pitcher, 8.5" tall, 1/2 gal., 1931 to 1935, **$1400**

Moongleam, Warwick #1428, Horn of Plenty, Vase, 9" tall, 7.5" long, 1933 to 1935, **$675**

Moongleam, Jamestown #3408, Beer Mug, Moongleam handle, 4" tall, 1933 to 1935, **$195**

Original advertising, Glass Secrets Series, "Marietta Betrays the Secrets of Colored Glass", from Good Housekeeping May 1928, features Moongleam color

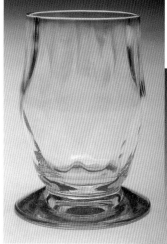

Moongleam, Glenford #3481, Tumbler, 2.5" tall, Moongleam foot, 1925 to 1935, **$38**

Moongleam, Ball #4045, Vase, Wide Optic, 6.5" tall, 1935, **$800**

Moongleam, Seven Octagon #4035, Cologne, Duck stopper, 4.5" tall, 1929 to 1933, **$450**

Moongleam, Steeple Chase #4224, Cocktail, 4" tall, Moongleam satin base, 1931 to 1935, **$60**

Moongleam, #4224, Ivy vase, 4.5" tall, Arctic etching, 1932 to 1935, **$250**

Moongleam, Diamond Optic, favor vases, 1925 to 1935
Left to Right: #4227, 3" tall, **$425**; #4228, 3" tall, **$625**; #4229, 3" tall, **$400**; #4230, 3", **$400**; #4231, 3" tall, **$410**; #4232, 3" tall, **$525**

OPAL

Opal was an opaque white glass introduced in 1898 and was more commonly called "Milk Glass." The name was given in the early days because of its resemblance to milk. When held up to a strong light, *Opal* takes on a fiery opalescence that resembles the natural stone opal. One of the major patterns Heisey used in *Opal* was the Beaded Swag pattern. Heisey developed a whole tableware line decorated with flowers utilizing enamel paints. Other companies purchased *Opal* items and decorated them with an advertisement for the place of purchase as a souvenir. *Opal* was made for a short period of time and our best estimate is that this color ended about 1904.

Milk Glass was made at all the glass companies. It was probably most popular at Fenton, in their Hobnail line, and at Westmoreland, in their Paneled Grape and Old Quilt lines. Fenton changed their formula in the 1950s to be more white. Fenton's first milk glass looked very close to Heisey's *Opal*.

Opal, Beaded Swag #1295, Covered Butter, 5.25" tall, 7.25" wide, 1899 to 1903, **$125**

Opal, Punty Band #1220, Creamer, 2.75" tall, souvenir Lake Michigan Park, Muskegon, Mich., 1897 to 1909, **$35**

Opal, Beaded Swag #1295, Spooner, 4" tall, floral decoration, 1899 to 1903, **$75**

Opal, Beaded Swag #1295, hand painted pink flowers, 1899 to 1903, **Left:** spooner, 4" tall, **$65**, **Right:** covered sugar, 6" tall, **$75**

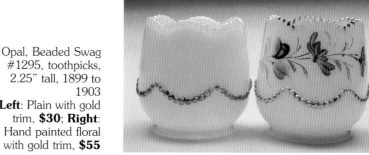

Opal, Beaded Swag #1295, toothpicks, 2.25" tall, 1899 to 1903 **Left**: Plain with gold trim, **$30**; **Right**: Hand painted floral with gold trim, **$55**

SAHARA

Sahara was a light, transparent, yellow color that was produced to replace *Marigold*, that had failed so badly. Introduced in 1929, *Sahara* was instantly popular with the public. Heisey made headlines in the trade journals with *Sahara* because it was the first yellow with a lead base. Olson listed it in his notebook as "Lead Sahara."

The name was derived from the sands of the Sahara desert. The beautiful yellow color proved to have a stable formula and the color was easily maintained. Sahara was discontinued in 1937. Full place settings can be gathered in Empress, Ipswich, Old Sandwich, and Yeoman.

Topaz was a beautiful color for Fostoria that closely resembled *Sahara*. Cambridge had the similar color *Gold Krystol* that sold well for them.

Sahara, #18, Flower Frog, 9" long, oval, fits inside Trident bowl, 1930 to 1937, **$145**

Sahara, Short Panel #23, Shakers, 2.5" tall, 1929 to 1937, **$80 pair**

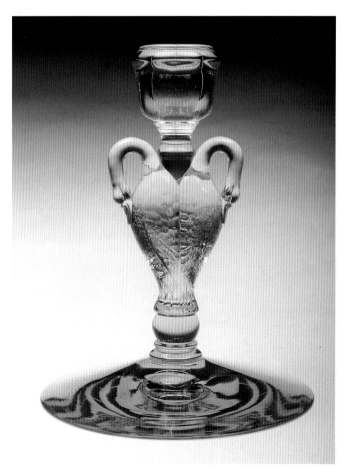

Sahara, Swan #133, Candlestick, 6.75" tall, 1929 to 1936, **$200**

Sahara, Trident #134, Floral
cutting, 1930 to 1937
Left: Floral bowl, 14" long,
7.5" wide, **$195**; **Right**: Duo
Candlestick, 6" tall, 6.5" wide,
$75

Sahara,Trident #134, Floral bowl, 14" long,
7.5" wide, 1930 to 1937, **$150**

Sahara, Gascony #138, Candlestick, 6.5" tall, 1931 to 1936, **$160**

Sahara, Old Williamsburg
#300-1, Candelabra, 11.5"
tall, 1929 to 1937, **$300**

Sahara, Winston #360, Match stand ashtray, 2.75" tall, 6" wide, 1929 to 1937, **$45**

Sahara, McGrady #372, Sanitary Syrup, 3" tall, 5 ounce, 1929 to 1937, **$125**

Sahara, McGrady #372, Syrup, 5" tall, 1929 to 1937, **$165**

Original advertising, "Alluring Etched Glass by Heisey...the most expressive gift", from House and Garden November 1930, featured Old Colony

Sahara, Old Colony, etching #448, 1930 to 1937
Left: Vase, 9.5" tall, dolphin footed, **$150**;
Back Right: Tray, 13" wide, sandwich, **$80**
Front Right: Cup, 2.6" tall, 6 ounce, Saucer, 6.5" wide, **$75**

Sahara, Petal #479, 1929 to 1935
Left: Sugar, 4" tall, **$95**; **Right**: Creamer, 4.25" tall, **$85**

Sahara, Octagon #500, 1929 to 1935
Left: Sugar, 2.5" tall, **$45**; **Right**: Creamer, 2.5"
tall, **$40**

Sahara, Yeoman #1184, Creamer,
2.75" tall, 1929 to 1937, **$45**

Sahara, Yeoman #1184, Diamond Optic, 1929 to 1937
Left: Covered Sugar, 3.5" tall, **$60**; **Right**: Creamer, 3" tall, **$45**

Right:
Sahara, Yeoman #1184, Covered
Mustard with spoon, 3.75" tall,
1929 to 1937, **$295**

Sahara, Yeoman #1189, Individual, 1929 to 1937
Left: Covered Sugar, 3.75" tall, **$95**; **Right**:
Creamer, 2.75" tall, **$75**

Sahara, Ribbed Octagon #1231, 1929 to 1936
Left: Sugar, 3.25" tall, **$40**; **Right**: Creamer, 3.25" tall, **$35**

Sahara, Beehive #1238, Plate, 8" wide, 1929 to 1937, **$75**

Sahara, Twist #1252, Bowl, 8" wide, Nasturtium, 1929 to 1937, **$100**

Sahara, Twist #1252, Covered Candy, three corner mint, 3.75" tall, 6.5" wide, 1929 to 1937, **$80**

Sahara, Twist #1252, Oval Hotel, 1929 to 1937
Left: Sugar, 3.25" tall, **$60**; **Right**: Creamer, 4.25" tall, **$60**

Sahara, Empress #1401, Punch
cup, 2.25" tall, 1930 to 1937, **$30**

Sahara, Empress #1401, 1930 to
1937, **$110 set**
Back: Tray, 6" wide, 11" long;
Front Left: Sugar, 3" tall; **Front
Right**: Creamer, 3.25" tall

Sahara, Half Circle #1403, 1930 to 1935
Left: Sugar, 2.75" tall, **$50**; **Right**: Creamer, 2.75" tall, **$50**

Sahara, Old Sandwich #1404, 1931 to 1937
Left: Sugar, 2.75" tall, **$46**; **Right**: Creamer, 3" tall, **$46**

Sahara, Victorian #1425, 1933
Left: Sugar, 3" tall, **$60**; **Right**: Creamer, 3" tall, **$60**

Sahara, Warwick #1428, Horn of Plenty vases, 1933 to 1937
Left: Medium 7" tall, **$450**; **Center**: Small 5" tall, **$395; Right**: Large 9" tall, **$480**

Sahara, Crystolite #1503, 1937
Left: Ashtray, 3" wide, **$35**; **Right**: Covered Cigarette box, 2.5" tall, 4" long, 3.5" wide, **$98**

Sahara, Aristocrat
#1430, Covered candy,
13" tall, .5 pound, 1933
to 1937, **$950**

Sahara, Duquesne #3389, Soda Tumbler, 5" tall, 12 ounce, Chintz #450 etching, 1930 to 1937, **$19.50**

Sahara, Old Dominion #3380, Water Goblet, 8" tall, 10 ounce, 1930 to 1937, **$28**

Sahara, Ball #4045, Vase, 5.5" tall, 1936 to 1937, **$110**

Sahara, #4224, Ivy Vase, 4.5" tall, 1932 to 1937, **$125**

Sahara, Diamond Optic, favor vases, 1933 to 1937
Left to Right: #4227, 3" tall, **$230**; #4228, 3" tall, **$300**; #4229, 3" tall, **$185**;
#4230, 3" tall, **$320**; #4231, 3" tall, **$275**; #4232, 3" tall, **$280**

STIEGEL BLUE

Stiegel Blue is a dark transparent, blue color that was introduced in 1932. Today, many collectors refer to it as "Cobalt." It is a very rich color that has Cobalt Black Oxide, Powdered Blue, and Black Oxide Copper as part of the formula. Many items were made in *Stiegel Blue,* including the patterns Empress, Ipswich, Old Sandwich, and Victorian. Numerous stems were also made in *Stiegel Blue* and *Crystal,* as an attractive combination. Some thick pieces of *Stiegel Blue* are so intense that you can barely see any light through them. Stiegel Blue was discontinued in 1941.

All of the major elegant glass companies, such as Cambridge, Duncan, Fenton, Fostoria, Imperial, and Tiffin, produced this rich-looking glass. Some inexpensive Depression era glassware also was made in a color also called *Cobalt,* but the Depression era *Cobalt* is pale and much less intense than Heisey's *Stiegel Blue.*

Stiegel Blue, Empress #135, Candlesticks, 6.5" tall, 1932 to 1937, **$950 pair**

Stiegel Blue, Ribbed Octagon #1231, Rum Pot, 7" tall, 7.5" wide, 1932 to 1933, **$3200**

Stiegel Blue, Empress #1401,
Covered Candy, 5.75" tall, 6.5"
wide, 1930 to 1938, **$500**

Stiegel Blue, Empress #1401,
Square Plate, 8.5" wide,
1930 to 1938, **$95**

Stiegel Blue, Old Sandwich #1404, 1932 to 1941
Left: Sherry Bottle, 8.5" tall, Crystal stopper, **$950**; **Right**: Tumbler, 2" tall, two ounce, bar, **$95**

Stiegel Blue
Left: Ipswich #1405, Bowl, Floral, footed, 11" wide, 1932 to 1938, **$345**
Center: Advertising plaque;
Right: Ipswich #1405, Footed centerpiece with vase and prisms, two piece with candle cup, **$650**

Stiegel Blue, Cathedral #1413, Vase, 8" tall, 1932 to 1941, **$675**

Stiegel Blue, 20th Century #1415, Tumbler,
4.75" tall, 9 ounce, 1932 to 1937, **$85**

Stiegel Blue, Tulip #1420, Vase, 9" tall, 1933 to 1937, **$725**

Stiegel Blue, Hi Lo #1421, Vase, 8" tall,
1933 to 1937, **$750**

Stiegel Blue, Victorian #1425, Bowl, 10.5" wide,
1933 to 1939, **$300**

Stiegel Blue, Warwick #1428,
Vase, Horn of Plenty, 1933 to
1941
Left: Large 9" tall, **$395**;
Center: Medium 5" tall, **$300**;
Right: Small 2" tall, **$85**

Stiegel Blue, Pristine #1429, Floral Bowl, 12.5"
long, 1933 to 1938, **$300**

Stiegel Blue, Aristocrat #1430, Covered Candy,
10.75" tall, 1933 to 1937, **$1950**

Stiegel Blue, Morse #1476, Torte Plate,
18.5" wide, 1935 to 1937, **$500**

Stiegel Blue, Wampum #1533, Floral Bowl, 9.5" wide, 1941, **$2500**

Stiegel Blue, Navy #2323, 1934 to 1941 **Left**: Plate, 6" wide, **$45**;
Center: Bar Tumbler, 2.5" tall, **$75**; **Right**: Plate, 8.25" wide, **$75**

Stiegel Blue, Navy #2323, Tumblers, 1934 to 1941
Top Left: 2.5" tall, **$75**; Top Right: 3.6" tall, **$45**
Bottom Left to Right: 8" tall, **$150**; 3.5" tall, **$40**; 3.35"
tall, **$35**; 5.75" tall, 12 ounce, **$60**

Stiegel Blue, Carcassonne
#3390, Cigarette holder,
Stiegel Blue bowl, 3.25" tall,
1932 to 1941, **$145**

Stiegel Blue, Gascony #3397,
Decanter, 11" tall, one pint,
Crystal stopper and foot,
1932 to 1938, **$975**

Original label: Old Century
Spanish, Silver and Blue foil

Stiegel Blue, Spanish #3404, Stiegel Blue bowl, 1933
Left: Comport, 6" tall, 6" wide, **$650**;
Right: Tumbler, soda, 6.25" tall, 12 ounce, **$85**

Stiegel Blue, Jamestown #3408, Beer Mug, 4" tall, 12 ounce, Stiegel Blue handle,
1933 to 1941, **$200**

Stiegel Blue, New Era #4044, Tumbler,
Stiegel Blue bowl, 6.5" tall, 1934, **$150**

Stiegel Blue, Ball #4045, Wide Optic, vases, 1936 to 1941
Top Center: 11.5", **$2400; Top Right**: 6.5" tall, **$750**
Bottom Left: 8" tall, **$950**; **Center**: 5.5" tall, **$500**;
Right: 3.5" tall, **$225**

Stiegel Blue, Ball shaker,
embossed swimming fish
on sides, 2.25" tall,
**Market price undeter-
mined**
Note: This item was
purchased at the Gus
Heisey auction

Stiegel Blue, #4224, Ivy Vase, 4.5" tall,
1932 to 1937, **$95**

Stiegel Blue, Diamond Optic, favor vases, 1933 to 1941
Left to Right: #4227, 3" tall, **$225**; #4228, 3" tall, **$185**; #4229, 3" tall, **$195**; #4230, 3" tall, **$225**; #4231, 3" tall, **$175**; #4232, 3" tall, **$250**

TANGERINE

Tangerine debuted in 1932 and was made until 1935. This is a vibrant transparent orange that resembles the tangerine fruit. *Tangerine* is a heat-sensitive glass, since it starts out as a yellow color and upon reheating changes to orange. Some almost red pieces have been found, leading some collectors to believe they have found a new color. In reality, they were overheated and changed a very dark color of *Tangerine*. Because of production problems in maintaining this color, *Tangerine* was discontinued three years after it was introduced. It sometimes take on a reddish amber color, as in the Trident double candlesticks.

During the 1930s, an orange colored glass that resembles *Tangerine* was imported from Czechoslovakia. An ivy ball vase has been frequently mistaken for Heisey. Fenton also made a *Tangerine* color that is lighter and more transparent. In the photographs shown here, you will see a wide variety of color.

Tangerine, Trident #134, Duo candle holder, 5.5" tall, 6.5" wide, base is Crystal, 1932 to 1935, **$650**

Tangerine, Empress #1401, Bowl with dolphin feet, 11" wide, 1932 to 1935, **$3000**

Tangerine, Gascony #3397, Bowl, 10" wide, Crystal base, 1932 to 1935, **$1450**

Tangerine, Gascony #3397, Tumbler, 5.5" tall, 1932 to 1935, Crystal base, **$140**
Left: Dark color; **Right**: Light color

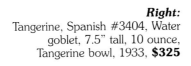

Right:
Tangerine, Spanish #3404, Water goblet, 7.5" tall, 10 ounce, Tangerine bowl, 1933, **$325**

Tangerine, Jamestown #3408, Beer mug, 4" tall, 12 ounce, Tangerine handle, 1933 to 1935, **$250**

Tangerine, #4224, Ivy ball vase, 4.5" tall, 1932 to 1935, **$150**

Tangerine Favor vases, Diamond Optic, 1933 to 1935
Left to Right: #4231, 3.15" tall, **$400**; #4232, 3" tall, **$400**; #4230, 3" tall, **$600**; #4227, 3" tall, **$625**

ZIRCON AND LIMELIGHT

Zircon was introduced in 1936 and made for three years. This was the last new color Heisey introduced before World War II. It is a pale transparent, blue-green tint that somewhat resembles turquoise. In Olson's formula book, there were five versions of *Zircon*, depending on the levels of chemicals added. These were listed as a *Green Side*, *Blue Side*, *Blue 1st*, *Blue 2nd*, and *Green 3rd*.

The formula was altered and renamed *Limelight* when it was reissued in 1955. The *Zircon* formula had quantities of Powdered Blue increased, and the amounts for Copper Scale and Green Oxide of Chrome decreased. The adjusted formula was given a new name to give the color fresh appeal. There were production problems in maintaining the uniformity of this color and some pieces look more ultramarine, while others look darker green. The color was still available when the company closed in 1957.

After the end of World War I, the Moser Company of Czechoslovakia developed 22 new, non-rare earth colors. In 1921, their new color *Beryl* made its debut as a transparent color with a turquoise tint. This color very closely resembles *Zircon*, the light green color that Heisey would later develop. The two colors are strikingly similar. It is not known where Heisey obtained their formula, but Moser developed their color first. Perhaps the same European source for the *Alexandrite* formula provided the formula for *Zircon*.

Beryl, Vase, Wide Panels, 5.75" tall, Made by Moser, marked with acid signature of Moser KarlovyVary, 1921, **$300**

Zircon, Rococo #1447, five part utility relish, 10" wide, 1936 to 1939, **$850**

Zircon, Ridgleigh #1469, 1936 to 1939
Left: Footed Vase, 4.5" tall, **$160**; **Center**: Coaster, 3.5" wide, **$125**; **Right**: Vase, 8" tall, **$575**

Zircon, Saturn #1485, 1936 to 1939
Left: Oval bowl, 2.6" tall, 6" long, **$100**; **Center**: Cruet, 6.5" tall, **$350**; **Right**: Shaker, 3.2" tall, **$95**

Zircon, Saturn #1485, Salad bowl, 10.5" wide, 1936 to 1939, **$250**

Zircon, Saturn #1485, 1936 to 1939
Left: Single Candlestick, 3.5" tall, **$195**; **Right**: Duo Candlestick, 5.5" tall, 8" wide, **$650**

Original Heisey brochure advertising Saturn

Zircon, Saturn #1485, Duo Candle Block,
2.5" tall, 7.25" long, 1936 to 1939, **$350**

Zircon, Saturn #1485, Cup, 2.5" tall,
Saucer, 6" wide, 1936 to 1939, **$125**

Zircon, Saturn #1485, 1936 to 1939
Back: Plate, 7.25" wide, **$100**
Front Left to Right: Goblet, 5.5" tall, **$125**; Tumbler, 5.25" tall, 8 ounce, **$160**; Sherbet, 4.5" tall, 4.5 ounce, **$60**

Zircon, Saturn #1485, 1936 to 1939
Left: Vase, 7" tall, **$250**;
Right: Comport, 6.25" tall, 7.5" wide, **$100**

Zircon, Saturn #1485, Hostess Helper, metal insert to hold toothpicks, 12.5" wide, center bowl, flat, 4.25" wide, 1936 to 1939, **$300**

Zircon, Saturn #1485, Hostess Helper, bowl 12.5" wide, center crystal footed bowl, 4.75" wide, with crystal toothpick holders, original box in background, 1936 to 1939, **$300**
Note: Crystal bowl in center is not original

Zircon, Saturn #1485, Covered Mustard
with paddle, 4" tall, 1936 to 1939, **$500**

Zircon, Saturn #1485, 1936 to 1939
Left: Vase, 8.4" tall, **$275**; **Right**: Pitcher, 7.75" tall, **$950**

Zircon, Saturn #1485, 1936 to 1939
Left: Sugar, 2.4" tall, **$125**; **Right**: Creamer, 2.5" tall, **$125**

Zircon, Saturn #1485, 1936 to 1939
Left: Vase, 7.75" tall, **$225**; **Right**: Rose Bowl, 6.25" tall, **$325**

Zircon, Saturn #1485, 1936 to 1939
Left: Violet Vase, 2.75" tall, **$175**; **Right**: Mayonnaise, 4" wide, **$100**

Zircon, Kohinoor #1488, two light Candelabra, 4.5" tall, 10.5" long, Crystal bobeches and prisms, 1937 to 1939, **$1750**

Left:
Zircon, Kohinoor #1488, 1937 to 1939
Left: Tumbler, 5.75" tall, 12 ounce, crystal top with Zircon base, **$200**; **Right**: Goblet, 7.75" tall, 9 ounce, Zircon bowl with Crystal stem and foot, **$195**

Zircon, Kohinoor #1488, Ball Vase, 8" tall, 1937 to 1939, **$750**

Zircon, Fern #1495, 1937 to 1939
Back: Three-part Relish,12.5" long, 7" wide, **$220**
Note: The jello is the same as the relish without the divisions
Front Left: two part mayonnaise, 5" wide, **$300**; **Front Right**: Tid bit plate, 6" long, **$245**

Zircon, Crystolite #1503, 1938 to 1939
Left: Ashtray, 3" wide, **$60**; **Right**: Covered Cigarette box, 2.5" tall, 4" long, **$250**

Left:
Zircon, Whirlpool #1506, Covered Candy,
8.5" tall, 5" wide, 1938 to 1939, **$375**

Zircon, Whirlpool #1506, 1938 to 1939
Back: 4 part Relish, handled, 11.5" long, 7.5" wide, **$150**
Front Left: Tumbler, 4" tall, 8 ounce, **$100**; **Front Center**: Bowl,
4.25" wide, **$60**; Front **Right**: Tumbler, 4.25" tall, 9 ounce, **$125**

Zircon, Whirlpool #1506,
1938 to 1939
Back: Plate, 8" wide, **$50**
Front Left: Sugar, 3.5" tall,
$100; **Front Right**: Creamer,
3.75" tall, **$100**

Limelight, Town and Country #1637, Salad set, 1955 to 1957, **$350**
Bowl, 11" wide; Plate, 14.25" wide

Limelight, Cabochon #1951, Covered Candy, 4.25" tall, 6.75" wide, 1955 to 1957, **$495**
Note: This was the last major pattern produced by Heisey before their closure.

Zircon, Cecelia #4057, Vase, 10.5" tall, 1936 to 1939, **$300**

Zircon, Carcassone #3390, Vase, 8.6" tall, Crystal stem and foot, 1936 to 1939, **$925**

Zircon, Stanhope #4083, 1936 to 1939
Left: Saucer Champagne, 4.4" tall, **$150**; **Right**: Water Goblet, 5.4" tall, **$195**

Limelight, Verlys, Chrysanthemum #V-1065, Window box, 10.25" long, 6" wide, satin finish, 1955, **$700**

Limelight, Verlys, Thistle #V8636, Bowl, 8.5" wide, satin finish, 1955, **$275**
Note: The bowl was taken upside down to show off pattern

2. EXPERIMENTAL COLORS

The following thirteen colors of glass were developed at Heisey, but were never put into production. Some were developed as variations of other colors, while others came about trying different combinations of chemicals. Also, sometimes the color in the glass pot became overheated resulting in a different color.

Because of the small amounts of ingredients used, "monkey pots" frequently were used in glassmaking to melt the chemicals. The name "monkey" refers to a small, 50-pound pot that usually sat on the edge of a larger pot. They were used for small batches, such as an experimental color, where limited amounts were being made.

Most of the following experimental colors were made in limited quantities and are rarely found in glass on the open market today. Therefore, for many, examples were not found to photograph. Without consistent sales on which to base a value, they all are listed here as "market value undetermined."

BLACK

Black was made only as an experimental color by Heisey in the early 1950s, when Heisey was also developing the color *Dawn*; it was not put into production. *Black* is cobalt based and was developed from the formula for *Stiegel Blue*. To have an example of this rare color would be a real treasure in your collection. Some of the pieces produced were: Colonial marmalade, Lariat salad plate, Priscilla under plate for the mayonnaise and Town & Country salad plate. While we call black a color, it is in fact not a color, but actually the absence of light being able to traverse through it. This gives you the illusion that the glass is in fact black. Most companies used amethyst to produce black. You could use almost any intense color, as Heisey did with cobalt or other glass companies did with green or red to produce a black.

For most of the glass companies of the time, black was a staple color and full lines of items were developed. Why Heisey chose not to produce *Black* is a real mystery.

CANARY OPALESCENT

At the time *Canary* was being made in the late 1890s, a sampling of pieces were made with an opalescent edge. Some pieces are known to exist in the Pineapple & Fan and Plaid patterns.

CRYSTAL OPALESCENT

Crystal Opalescent is a *Crystal* glass with a milky white accent. It has been found only in a few items from the 1890s to early 1900s.

DARK EMERALD

While *Emerald* was being made in 1896, the formula was darkened to make an almost black shade. Only a few pieces of *Dark Emerald* are known to exist. It is a very rare color.

EXPERIMENTAL BLUE

A light blue color known as *Experimental Blue* was designed as an addition to Heisey's palate for special orders. It was apparently developed to compete with the successful *Moonlight Blue* at Cambridge, but for some reason was never put into production. It was made during the 1930s.

A light blue color called *Moonlight Blue* was very popular and sold well for Cambridge Glass. *Aquamarine* was a beautiful light blue color at Fenton. Fostoria Glass produced an *Azure Blue* in many of their patterns. At New Martinsville, *Sky Blue* was very popular. *Copen Blue* was popular at Tiffin.

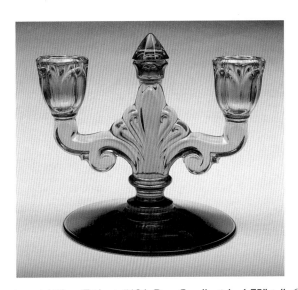

Experimental Blue, Trident #134, Duo Candlestick, 4.75" tall, 6.5" long, 1930s,
Market price undetermined

Experimental Blue, Ridgeleigh #1469, Star Relish, 9.5" long, 1930s, **Market price undetermined**

Experimental Blue, Ball #4045, Vase, 2" tall, 1930s, **Market price undetermined**

Experimental Blue, Morse #1476, Torte Plate, 18.5" wide, 1930s, **Market price undetermined**

GOLD

Gold is a Heisey experimental color that was a pale version of the *Marigold* dating from the late 1920s. Under a black light this color will fluoresce orange. Not many pieces of *Gold* are known.

GOLD OPALESCENT

Gold Opalescent is Heisey's *Gold* with opalescent coloring on the edges. It is another experimental color that was not put into production. Only a few pieces of Gold Opalescent are known to exist.

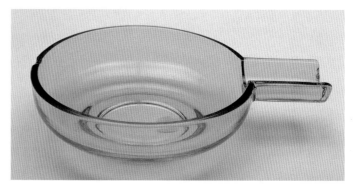

Gold, Solitaire #358, Stick Ashtray, 3" wide, 1920s, **Market price undetermined**

GOLD RUBY

Gold Ruby is another experimental color that was not put into production. It dates from the early 1930s. This color resembles Cranberry and has been frequently called this by Heisey collectors. Most pieces in *Gold Ruby* are in the hands of former Heisey employees.

Gold Ruby, #3966, Comport, 6.5" tall, 6" wide, #674 Adams cutting, Crystal stem and foot, early 1930s, **Market price undetermined**

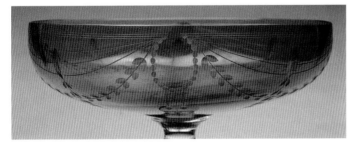

Gold Ruby, #3966, Comport, close-up of #674 Adams cutting

To obtain *Gold Ruby*, Heisey specialists first gathered Ruby glass and then cased it with Crystal glass. The molten glass was then blown into the desired mould. Once blown, the color took on a Cranberry color. As a case in point, the Fenton Art Glass Company put their version of this color glass in production in the 1940s and initially called it Ruby Overlay. Later, they renamed this glass Cranberry or Country Cranberry, since it was a more popular name.

INK BLUE

Ink Blue was a transparent teal blue color that was made at Heisey from the 1890s to the early 1900s. Only a few pieces were made.

MOONSTONE

Moonstone is a translucent opal color that was developed in 1940 as Emmit Olson was working with Carl Reed to develop the formula. A few stemware items have been found where the bowl and base are colored glass and the stem is *Moonstone*.

RED

It was first thought that some *Red* items were an overcooked version of *Tangerine*. But, according to Olson's notebook, a separate *Red* formula was being developed in 1934 and was made in a monkey pot. Correspondence from H. Schnurpfeil of Prague reveals that Olson obtained four glass formulas from him, one of which was *Red*. In a letter from George Blumenthal of Crown Chemical, we learn that the addition of Antimony to the batch reveals a more intense red. It appears that the *Red* color was used only for the handles of beer mugs.

Red, Jamestown #3408, Beer mug, Red handle, 1934, **Market price undetermined**

ROSE

Old inventory records have been brought to light that reveal a color of *Rose* being made around 1901 to 1903. A mystery had previously existed with some old patterns appearing in a pink color that did not match the time frame when *Flamingo* was introduced. *Rose* is a light pink transparent color similar to *Flamingo* but without the orange tint. Items in this early color are very hard to find. Some are: Peerless candlestick, several sizes of bowls in Pillows, and a Ring Band spoon holder.

TANGERINE OPALESCENT

While *Tangerine* was being produced in the early 1930s, some additions were made to the formula to enable it to take on a more opalescent appearance. The result was not liked as well as the transparent *Tangerine* and the decision was made to not offer a full line of items. Only a few examples were made.

Tangerine, Steele #4157, Rose bowl, 5.5" tall, Opalescent top rim, early 1930s, **Market price undetermined**

Tangerine, Olympia #4191, Bud vase, 11.75" tall, Crystal foot, early 1930s, **Market price undetermined**

Tangerine, Larson #8066, Bottle Vase, 6.5" tall, Experimental, early 1930s, **Market price undetermined**

VASELINE

When Heisey was developing the Visible Cookware in 1919, they used a yellow-green glass that will glow under a black light. They did not name this color, but since it contains the properties of Vaseline, we have listed it here as *Vaseline*. It is assumed that Heisey returned to its original *Canary* formula, adding the needed chemicals to make it oven-proof.

Vaseline, Visible Cooking Ware, Bowl, 9.75" wide, Marked with Diamond H mark, 1919, **Market price undetermined**
Note: This bowl is shown upright to reveal the Diamond H mark

Vaseline, Visible Cooking Ware, Bowl, 9.75" wide, Marked with Diamond H mark, 1919, **Market price undetermined**
Note: Heisey did not name this color but since it is a yellowish green, which defines Vaseline, we are listing it as Vaseline. It will glow under a black light.

3. THE DECORATING COMPANIES

A wide variety of companies decorated Heisey glass. The majority of Heisey glass had decorations applied by the following companies: Bonita Art, Central Glass, Lotus Glass, Oriental Glass, Rainbow Glass, Wheeling Decorating and many others. Other companies purchased Heisey blanks on which to cut or etch patterns, including Eagle Cut Glass, Hawkes, Monogram, Pairpoint, and Sinclair. Silver companies that utilized Heisey glass for silver overlay include Apollo, National Silver, Poole, Reed and Barton, and Tuttle. Pieces accented with metal ormolu also appear. Some were sold by the Apollo Metal Works of New York. While we have found several pieces that demonstrate the style and quality of Apollo, only two examples were marked.

Even though the glass was made by Heisey, the catalogs and advertisements of the decorating companies placed emphasis on their special decorations, and no mention was made of the maker of the glass. In addition, blanks made at different glass companies could be similarly decorated and then marketed together under a particular decorating company's label.

Unless you find an original advertisement listing the particular decoration, there is no way of specifically identifying the particular decorating company. A few did patterns that were unique to them, and thereby set their products apart from others.

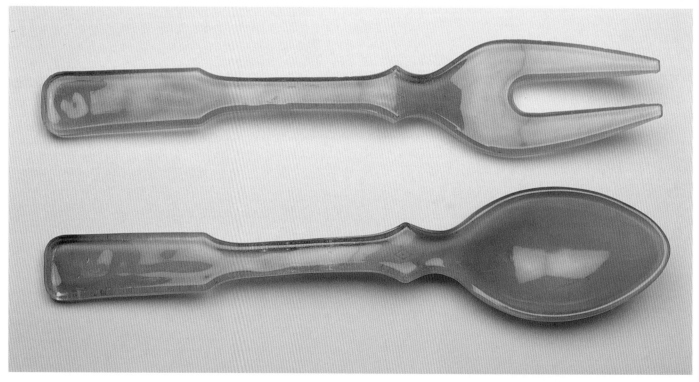

Green Fired-on, #2, Salad fork and spoon, Crystal, 1940s
Top: Spoon, 10" long, 2.25" wide; **Bottom**: Fork, 10.1" long, 2" wide, **$125 pair**

Green Fired-on, detail of Heisey
mark on the Salad fork

Crystal, Stanford #29, Candlestick, 9.5" tall, metal ormolu at top and bottom, possibly Chicago Brass, 1920s, **$95**

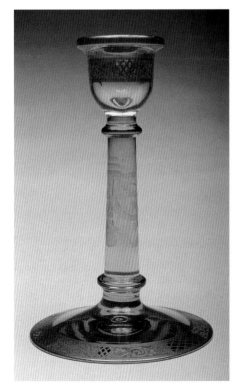

Moongleam, Wellington #107, Candlestick, 10" tall, Silver floral band at top and bottom, 1930s, **$295**

Crystal, Centennial #100, Candlestick, 6" tall, Marigold stain, Gold encrusted band at top and bottom, Hawkes decoration, 1920s, **$85**

Ruby Flash, toothpicks,1910s
Left: Prince of Wales #335, 2.5" tall, Fairfield, Iowa etching,
$250; **Right**: Punty Band #1220, 2.25" tall, Monticello, Minn.
etching, **$60**

Crystal with Gold Flash, Narrow Flute #394, Cracker and Cheese,
4.25" tall, 9.5" wide, silver trim, 1910s, **$60**

Crystal with Gold Flash, Coarse Rib #406, Mustard
Jar, 3.8" tall, 1920s to 1930s, **$48**

Crystal, Narrow Flute #393, Covered Candy, 7" tall, 5.5" wide, footed,
gold band at top, crackle finish, "Fingered Swirls, Arrows and Flowers,"
decoration by Wheeling Decorating Company, 1910s, **$75**

Crystal, Tudor #411, Marigold stain, Silver overlay, 1930s
Left: Cigarette box with ashtray on top, 4.25" tall, **$98**; **Right**: Cigarette box, 4.75" tall, **$85**

Hawthorn, Petal #479, floral cutting, 1927 to 1935
Left: Sugar, 4" tall, **$115**; **Right**: Creamer, 4.25" tall, **$95**

Original label Heisey Made Athena Susquemanna Cut, Susquemanna Glass Co., Columbia, Pennsylvania

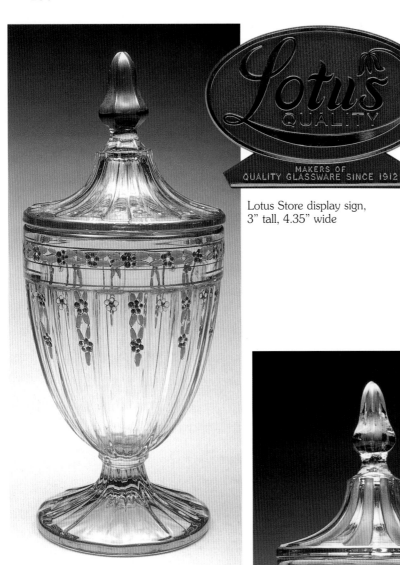

Lotus Store display sign,
3" tall, 4.35" wide

Crystal, Recessed Panel #465, Covered
candy, 10.5" tall, 4.5" wide, gold band
on edge and finial, enameled flowers,
possibly decorated by Lotus, 1930s, **$85**

Crystal, Recessed Panel #465, Covered
candy, 13" tall, 6" wide, "Double Con-
nected Roses", decoration by Wheeling
Decorating Company, 1930s, **$95**

Crystal, Recessed Panel #465, Covered candy,
10.5" tall, 4.5" wide, Ruby flashing on alternate
panels, gold trim on finial and bottom, 1930s,
$65

Crystal, Revere #1183, Covered Candy, 8" tall, 4.5" wide, blue floral band at top, "Fingered Swirls, Arrows and Flowers", decoration by Wheeling Decorating Company, 1930s, **$60**

Crystal, Hartman #469, Covered Candy, 10.5" tall, 4.5" wide, Silver trim, geometric cutting, 1920s, **$125**

Crystal, Revere #1183, Covered Sugar, 7" tall, 5" wide, green accents, black with yellow floral, footed, 1940s, **$95**

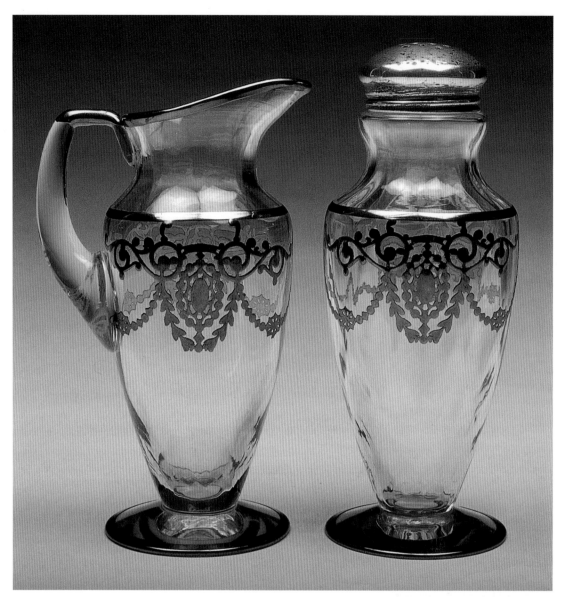

Crystal, Yeoman #1184, Moongleam handle and base, Silver Overlay of a Cameo with Swag
Left: Creamer, 5.6" tall, **$65**;
Right: Sugar Shaker, 5.9" tall, **$98**

Crystal with Gold Flash, Yeoman #1185, Covered candy box, flat, 3.5" tall, 6.25" wide, 1930s, **$75**
Note: The finial is actually Crystal but takes on the gold color when photographed.

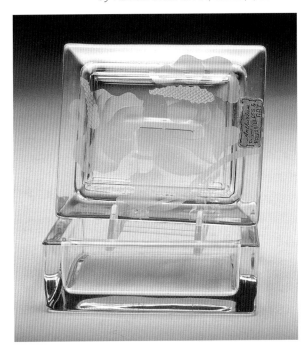

Crystal, Puritan #1489, Cigarette box,
1.5" tall, 4.24" long, floral decoration
original label says: Anthurium Designed
by Hawaii Glass & Art, 1950s, **$48**

Crystal, Yeoman #1185, Covered candy box, flat, 3.5" tall, 6.25"
wide, pastel iridized finish and white enamel flowers, 1930s, **$60**

Crystal, Puritan #1489 1/2, Horse Head, Cigarette box, 6.26" long, 4" wide, Ruby flash, 1950s, **$175**

Crystal, Crystolite #1503, Bookends utilizing flower candy lid, 4" tall, 6.5" long, 1950s, **$75 pair**

Crystal, Crystolite #1503, 1950s
Left & Right: Cologne w/drip stopper (dauber) 5.75", cylindrical, 4 ounce; **Center**: Box w/cover 4.75", puff, 4.1" tall; handled tray, 12.25" long. Cologne bottles and puff box each have ornate metal filigree on them to match the tray. On the bottom of the tray, it is marked Apollo. **$495**

APOLLO
A 1 4 0 5

Close-up of
Apollo mark

Crystal, Queen Anne #1509, Ice Tub, 6.75" tall, 5" wide, Fruit Sterling Overlay, 1950s, **$95**

Silver City Store Display sign, 2.5" tall, 5.25" long

Crystal, Waverly #1519, Shakers, 4" tall, Floral Silver Overlay, decoration by Silver City Glass Company, 1950s, **$28 pair**

Crystal, Lariat #1540, Bowl, 7.25" wide, Charleton decoration by Abels Wasserburg, **$45**

Original Charleton label

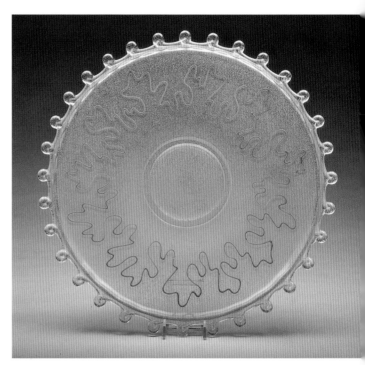

Crystal, Lariat #1540, Sandwich Plate, 14" wide, Pink splatter background with applied pink squiggles, **$75**

Crystal, Lariat #1540, Sandwich Plate, 14" wide, Charleton decoration by Abels Wasserburg Co, 1940s, **$95**

Crystal, Lariat #1540, Sandwich Plate, 14" wide, Sail boat Silver Overlay, **$125**

Crystal, Lariat #1540, Floral etch with stains, decoration by Farber Brothers, 1950s; some items had a gold foil label that read, "Coin Gold Farberware Brooklyn, NY"
Left: Sugar, 2.75" tall, **$24**; **Right**: Creamer, 3.3" tall, **$24**

Original Rockwell Silver label

Crystal, Lariat, #1540, Silver Overlay, Decorated by Rockwell Silver
Left: Sugar, 3" tall, **$18**; **Right**: Creamer, 3.25" tall, **$18**

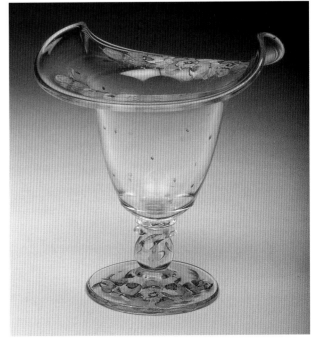

Crystal, Lariat #1540, Vase, 5.75" tall, Charleton decoration by Abels Wasserburg, 1940s, **$75**
Note: This is the basket shape missing the handle.

Crystal, satin finish, Silver Overlay with flying bird, Silver City Decorating
Left: Lariat #1540, Vase, 7.5" tall, **$75**;
Right: Victorian #1425, Match holder ashtray, 2.5" tall, 3" long, 1950s, **$48**

Crystal, Fish Bowl #1550, 9" tall, 9" long, Ruby Flash decoration, Designed by Royal Hickman, 1950s, **$950**

Crystal, Fish Bookends #1554, 6.75" tall, 5" long, Charleton, decoration by Abels Wasserburg Co., 1940s, **$395 pair**

Original Label of Warsaw Cut Glass Company of Indiana

Crystal, Lariat #5040, Goblet, 5.8" tall, 10 ounce, Blown, Wheat cutting by Warsaw Cut Glass Co., 1947 to 1957, **$35**

Crystal, Wreath #7004, Covered candy, 3.5" tall, 6.5" wide, metal embossed lid, possibly Chicago Brass,1950s, **$85**

=Collectors' Organizations=

No matter what pattern you collect, we encourage you to belong to a collector's organization and subscribe to a national glass publication. Each works to preserve the history of the American glassmaking industry. Whatever resource you use will enable you to gather more information on a particular glass topic. Each nonprofit organization provides information by publishing an educational newsletter, including study guides, reprinting company catalogs, conducting seminars, holding a convention, having a museum, or presenting other educational activities. An independent researcher, J. R. Schonscheck, has worked very hard over the last several years to offer a glass newsletter.

Glasstown USA
Attention: JR Schonscheck
5216 63rd St.
Kenosha, WI 53142
262-652-9749 or 262-358-0801
$12/year   6 newsletters a year
Web site: glasstown_usa@yahoo.com

Heisey Collectors of America
169 West Church Street, Newark, OH 43055
740-345-2932
$25/year   12 newsletters a year
Annual convention in June
Web site: www.heiseymuseum.org

West Virginia Museum of American Glass
P. O. Box 574, Weston, WV 26452
304-269-5006
$25/year   4 newsletters a year
Annual convention in October
Web site: http://members.aol.com/wvmuseumofglass/
www.allaboutglass.org

BIBLIOGRAPHY

Books

Baldwin, Gary and Lee Carno. *Moser-Artistry in Glass 1857-1938*. Marietta, Ohio: Antique Publications, 1988

Baldwin, Gary. *Moser Artistic Glass Edition Two*. Marietta, Ohio: Glass Press, 1997

Bradley, Stephen H, Constance S. Ryan and Robert R. Ryan. *Heisey Stemware*. Newark, Ohio: Spencer Walker Press, 1976

Bredehoft, Neila. *Collector's Encyclopedia of Heisey Glass 1925 - 1938*. Paducah, Kentucky: Collector Books, 1986

Bredehoft, Neila and Tom. *Handbook of Heisey Cuttings*. St. Louisville, Ohio: Cherry Hill Publications, 1991

_____. *Heisey Glass 1896 - 1957*. Paducah, Kentucky: Collector Books, 2001

Bredehoft, Neila and Tom and Louise Ream. *Encyclopedia of Heisey Glassware Volume I Etchings and Carvings*. Newark, Ohio: Heisey Collectors of America, 1977

_____. *Addendum to Encyclopedia of Heisey Glassware Volume I Etchings and Carvings*. Newark, Ohio: Heisey Collectors of America, 1981

Burns, Mary Louise. *Heisey's Glassware of Distinction*. Grants Pass, Oregon: Mary Louise Burns, 1983

Cochran, Gordon. *Catalogue 56 CA 1909 reprint A. H. Heisey & Co*. Newark, Ohio: Heisey Collectors of America, 1993

_____. *Catalogue 81 Basket catalogue reprint A. H. Heisey & Co*. Newberg, Oregon: Headrick Buchdruckerei, 1994

_____. *Catalogue 102 1924 reprint A. H. Heisey & Co*. Newark, Ohio: Heisey Collectors of America, 1993

Coe, Debbie and Randy. *Glass Animals and Figurines*. Atglen, Pennsylvania: Schiffer Publishing, 2003

_____. *Elegant Glass: Early, Depression and Beyond*. Atglen, Pennsylvania: Schiffer Publishing, 2004

Coe-Hixson, Myra. *Glass Elephants*. Atglen, Pennsylvania: Schiffer Publishing, 2004

Conder, Lyle, *Collector's Guide to Heisey's Glassware for your Table*. Gas City: L & W Book Sales, 1984

Felt, Tom and Rich Stoer, *The Glass Candlestick Book Volume 2 Fostoria to Jefferson*. Paducah, Kentucky: Collector Books, 2003

Felt, Tom and Bob O'Grady. *Heisey Candlesticks, Candelabra and Lamps*. Newark, Ohio: Heisey Collectors of America, 1984

Hahn, Frank and Paul Kikeli. *Collector's Guide to Heisey and Heisey by Imperial Glass Animals*. Lima, Ohio: Golden Era Publications, 1991

Heisey, A. H. *Heisey's Glassware Company Catalog*. Newark, Ohio: A. H. Heisey Company, 1930s

Heisey, A. H. *Heisey's Company Catalog 14-B reprint*. Gas City, Indiana: L-W Promotions, 1973

Heisey, A. H. *Heisey' Company Catalog 109 reprint*. Gas City, Indiana: L-W Promotions, 1974

Heisey Collectors of America. *Catalogue 32 1953 reprint*. Newberg, Oregon: Headrick Buchdruckerei, 1994

_____. *Catalogue 56 CA. 1909 reprint*. Newark, Ohio: Heisey Collectors of America, 1993

_____. *Catalogue 76 1915 reprint*. Newark, Ohio: Heisey Collectors of America, 1982s

_____. *Catalogue 102 CA. 1924s reprint*. Newark, Ohio: Heisey Collectors of America, 1993

Rogove, Susan Tobier and Marcia Buan Steinhauer. *Pyrex by Corning A Collector's Guide*. Marietta, Ohio: Antique Publications, 1993

Six, Dean. *Lotus Glass Depression Glass & Far Beyond*. Atglen, Pennsylvania: Schiffer Publishing, 2005

Stout, Sandra. *Heisey on Parade*. Lombard, Illinois: Wallace-Homestead Book Company, 1985

Vogel, Clarence. *Heisey's First Ten Years 1896 - 1905*. Galion, Ohio: Fisher Printing Co., 1969

_____. *Heisey's Colonial Years 1906 - 1922*. Galion, Ohio: Fisher Printing Co., 1969

_____. *Heisey's Art and Colored Glass 1922 - 1942*. Galion, Ohio: Fisher Printing Co., 1970

_____. *Heisey's Early and Late Years 1896- 1958*. Galion, Ohio: Fisher Printing Co., 1970

Webster, James L. *Wheeling Decorating Company*. Paducah, Kentucky: Collector Books, 2003

Willey, Harold E. *Heisey's Deep Plate Etching, Etched and Carved, Pressed and Blown handmade Glassware*. Frazeysburg, Ohio: Harold E. Wiley, 1973

Yeakley, Virginia and Loren. *Heisey Glass in Color*. Newark, Ohio: Virginia and Loren Yeakley, 1970

_____. *Heisey Glass in Color Book II, Marietta*, Ohio: Richardson Printing Corp., 1978

Monographs

West Virginia Museum of American Glass. *Decorated Glass of the 1950s*. Weston, West Virginia: West Virginia Museum of American Glass, 2000

_____. *Heisey Glass Formulas and More* Weston, West Virginia: West Virginia Museum of American Glass, 2004

_____. *Heisey: Table Glass and How to Use It: A 1911 Handbook for the Hostess*. Weston, West Virginia: West Virginia Museum of American Glass, 1999

_____. *Lotus Glass Company Catalog of 1944*. Weston, West Virginia: West Virginia Museum of American Glass, 1999

_____. *Silver City Glass Company*. Weston, West Virginia: West Virginia Museum of American Glass, 2000

Newsletter

Heisey Collectors of America. *Heisey News*. Newark, Ohio: Heisey Collectors of America, 1980s to 2005

Auction

Apple Tree Auctions. *Catalog of Auction Results*. Newark, Ohio. Apple Tree Auctions, 2000 to 2005

INDEX

A
Acorn 70
Adams Cutting 173
Advertising 7, 10 to19, 21, 31, 33, 37, 39, 44, 48, 49, 50, 51, 52, 55, 61, 75, 86, 91, 102, 105, 113, 116, 117, 119, 121, 125, 132, 160
Alexandrite 18-23, 157
Almond 82, 90, 104
Amber 18, 24-28
Antarctic etching 43
Apollo Metal Works 176, 184
Arctic etching 42, 127
Aristocrat 43, 85, 138, 148
Ash Receiver 65
Ashtray 39, 45, 46, 50, 53, 58, 80, 112, 114, 131, 138, 166, 172, 179
Asiatic Pheasant 26, 32
Athena 52, 179

B
Ball 23, 54, 126, 139, 152, 165, 172
Bamboo 108
Banded Flute 33, 110
Baskets 50, 74, 75, 91, 101, 114, 115, 117
Beaded Panel and Sunburst 41
Beaded Swag 67, 128
Beehive 81, 135
Bertha 106
Beryl 157
Black 11, 171
Bookends 184, 189
Botannical 53
Bowls 19, 21, 29, 30, 42, 45, 47, 49, 51, 54, 58, 62, 63, 65, 77, 81, 121 to 124, 130, 135, 145, 147 to 149, 154, 158, 159, 167, 168, 170, 175, 186
Butter Dish 34, 37, 38, 52, 53, 61, 63, 66, 95, 128

C
Cabochon 49, 56, 61, 168
Canary 8, 18, 29, 30, 171, 175
Canary Opalescent 171
Candelabra 33, 105, 106, 130, 165
Candlesticks 20, 21, 26, 33, 44, 46, 58, 59, 68-71, 89, 100, 105-110, 121-124, 129, 130, 141, 153, 159, 160, 171, 177
Candy Box 30, 43, 45, 46, 51, 52, 59, 61, 77, 79, 84, 85, 90, 102, 103, 115, 118, 135, 138, 143, 148, 167, 168, 178, 180-183, 189
Cane and Bar 95
Carcassone 22, 150, 169
Caswell 77, 92
Cathedral 145
Cecelia 169
Centennial 177
Charleton 186, 187, 189
Charter Oak 70
Cherub 33, 69, 107
Chintz 139
Cigarette Box and Jars 45, 48, 72, 112, 114, 138, 166, 183
Cigarette Holder 65, 150
Circle 76
Clydesdale 31
Coarse Rib 90, 178
Coaster 45, 68, 158
Cologne 76, 87, 92, 116, 118, 126, 184
Colonial Cupped Scallop 40
Colonial Panel 37
Colonial Scalloped Top 38
Compote 32, 45, 47, 69, 93, 107, 123, 151, 161, 173
Continental 35
Concave Circle 110
Convex Circle 40
Coronation 55
Creamers 34-36, 38-42, 44, 45, 52, 59, 61, 62, 64, 66, 67, 71, 72, 77, 80-83, 90-92, 95-101, 104, 111, 113, 116-118, 120-123, 128, 133-137, 163, 167, 179, 182, 187
Cross Lined Flute 29
Cruet 35, 57, 78, 81-83, 104 , 158

Crystal 6-9, 17, 18, 22, 31-55, 141, 150, 153, 154, 165, 169, 173, 176-189
Crystal Opalescent 171
Crystollite 46, 47, 58, 138, 166, 184
Cup and Saucer 22, 47, 49, 77, 93, 122, 132, 160
Custard 95, 103
Cut Block 41, 96, 97

D
Daisy and Leaves 39
Dark Emerald 171
Dawn 18, 56-61, 171
Decanter 54, 150
Diamond H 7, 8, 16, 17, 145, 176
Diamond Optic 80, 88, 92, 94, 118, 119, 127, 134, 140, 153, 156
Dice Sugar Tray 116
Doe Head 24
Dolphin 21, 22, 26, 32, 45, 69, 107, 123, 132, 154
Double Rib and Panel 91, 114
Duck Perfume 87, 126
Duquesne 139

E
Elaine 87
Elephant 24, 25, 32, 39, 49
Emerald 6, 18, 62-67, 105, 171
Empress 20-22, 42, 43, 68, 82, 83, 123, 129, 136, 141, 143, 154
Experimental Blue 171, 172

F
Fancy Loop 62, 63
Fairacre 76, 118
Fandango 41
Fatima 39
Favor Vases 88, 127, 140, 153, 156
Fern 166
Filly 25
Fish 26, 188, 189
Flamingo 18, 68-89, 173
Flat Panel 111
Flower Frog 76, 89, 108, 129
Flying Mare 25
Fogg 76, 101
Footed Centerpiece 145
Frances 88
Frog Cheese Dish 102, 120

G
Gallagher 55
Gascony 54, 130, 150, 154, 155
Glass Secrets Series 75, 102, 117, 121, 125
Glenford 60, 126
Goblets 27, 35, 93, 122, 139, 155, 161, 165, 169, 189
Gold 172
Gold Opalescent 172
Gold Ruby 173
Goose 28, 31
Grape Leaf Square 115
Grecian Border/Greek Key 73

H
Half Circle 83, 137
Harding 40
Hartman 181
Harvey, Fred 24, 27
Hawthorne 18, 31, 89-94, 179
Heisey, Augustus 6, 7, 9, 31
Heisey, George 6, 7
Hexagon Stem 116
Hickman, Royal 9, 24-26, 188
Holophane 9
Honey Amber 24, 25
Horn of Plenty 84, 125, 138, 147
Horse 31, 46, 51, 183
Humidor 65, 111

I
Ice Tub 45, 122, 185
Ink Blue 173
Inside Scallop 30
Ipswich 84, 124, 129, 141, 145
Irwin 112
Ivorina Verde 6, 18, 95-99
Ivory 18, 95
Ivy Vases 127, 140, 152, 156

J
Jamestown 86, 125, 151, 155, 173
Janice 23

K
Kalonyal 53
Kohinoor 165
Koors 87, 94
Krall, Emil 9, 43, 54

L
Labels 7, 8, 14, 16, 17, 52, 53, 68, 75, 89, 151, 179, 183, 185-187, 189
Lariat 50, 51, 171, 186-189
Larson 174
Legionnaire 28
Liberty 100
Lil Squatter 68
Limelight 18, 157, 168, 170
Lion Head 42, 123
Locket on Chain 29
Lodestar 56, 58, 59
Logo 17, 49, 93, 145, 176

M
Marigold 18, 100-104, 129, 172
Marmalade 20, 36, 45, 52
Match Holder/Stand 65, 131, 188
Mayonnaise Bowl 60, 90, 164, 166
McGrady 72, 112, 131
Medium Flat Panel 27, 36, 37, 90
Mercury 70, 89, 108
Mermaid 54
Military Hat 50
Molasses Can 37
Moongleam 18, 68, 105-127, 177, 182
Moonglo 51, 55
Moonstone 173
Morse 148, 172
Mug, Beer 25, 49, 86, 125, 151, 155, 173
Mustard 34, 48, 72, 79, 82, 83, 114, 134, 163, 178

N
Narrow Flute 29, 30, 38, 113, 116, 178
National 55
Navy 149, 150
New Era 151

O
Oakleaf 68
Octagon 56, 75, 94, 101, 103, 117, 118, 133
Old Colony 132
Old Dominion 139
Old Sandwich 124, 129, 137, 141, 144
Old Williamsburg 33, 105, 130
Olson, Emmet 9, 24, 56, 89, 129, 157, 173
Olympia 174
Opal 6, 18, 128,
Orchid 9, 48
Overlapping Swirl 109

P
Paneled Cane 34
Patrician 105
Pembroke 106
Perfume 76, 87, 92, 118, 126, 184
Peerless 173
Petal 92, 133, 179
Petticoat Dolphin 32, 69, 107
Pheasant 26
Phyllis 118
Pillows 34, 173
Pin Tray 66
Pineapple and Fan 63-65, 98, 171
Pinwheel 89
Pinwheel and Fan 29, 63, 111
Pitcher 35, 36, 38, 40, 47, 55, 57, 58, 87, 93, 94, 124, 163
Plantation 52
Plates 27, 30, 42, 43, 47, 77, 81, 90, 93, 103, 122, 135, 143, 148, 149, 161, 166 to 168, 172, 186
Platter 104
Pleat and Panel 68, 77, 78, 118, 119
Plug Horse 25, 51
Pointed Oval in Diamond Point 62
Prince of Wales 35, 178
Priscilla 29, 171
Prison Stripe 37
Pristine 148
Punch Bowl 38, 73
Punch Cup 62, 64, 73, 79, 83, 95, 96, 99, 111, 128, 136
Punty Band 97, 99, 128, 178
Puritan 183

Q
Quator 72, 100, 111
Queen Anne 38, 49, 185

R
Raised Loop 38
Recessed Panel 29, 30, 115, 180
Relish 49, 52, 56, 58, 60, 104, 119, 122, 157, 166, 167, 172
Revere 78, 79, 180
Rib Optic 94
Ribbed Octagon 135, 142

Ridgeleigh 45, 158, 172
Ringed Band 95, 96, 99, 173
Riviere cutting 43
Rococo 157
Rooster 55
Rose 9, 49, 68, 173
Rose Bowl 94, 164, 174
Roundelay 56

S
Sahara 18, 19, 129-140
Salad Fork and Spoon 176
Saturn 57, 158-164
Screen Optic 60
Seahorse 28, 48
Seven Circle 87
Seven Octagon 126
Shakers 33, 45, 52, 57, 129, 152, 158, 185
Sherry Bottle 144
Short Panel 129
Shot Glass 55
Silver City Glass Company 185, 188
Silver Overlay 177-179, 182, 185-188
Sodas 27, 55, 56, 139, 151
Solitaire 172
Spanish 151, 155
Spooner 40, 62, 64, 67, 95, 128
Sportsman Silhouette 54
Stanford 177
Stanhope 44, 169
Star and Zipper 63
Steele 94, 174
Steeple Chase 127
Stiegel Blue 18, 33, 141-153, 171
Stitch 96
Straw Holders 37
Sugars 34-36, 38-42, 44, 45, 52, 62, 64, 71-73, 80-83, 90-92, 95, 97-100, 104, 111, 113, 116-118, 120, 121, 123, 128, 133-137, 163, 167, 179, 187
Sugar Shaker 77, 92, 182
Sultana 24, 25, 28
Sunburst 36
Swan 45, 129
Swirl Optic 60, 87
Syrup 72, 112, 131

T
Tally Ho Silhouette 55
Tangerine 18, 153-156, 173, 174
Tangerine Opalescent 174
Taper 76, 92, 118
Thistle 170
Thumbprint and Panel 86
Toothpick 63, 95, 99, 178
Town and Country 60, 168, 171
Tray 52, 80, 110, 123, 132, 136
Tricorn 70, 100, 109
Trident 19, 20, 129, 130, 153, 171
Triplex 71, 110
Tudor 72, 73, 90, 91, 113, 114, 179
Tumbler 27, 47, 53-56, 60, 63, 93, 126, 139, 144, 146, 149-151, 155, 161, 165, 167
Twentieth Century 56, 57, 146
Twist 42, 68, 81, 82, 103, 104, 109, 121, 122, 135, 136
Twist Stem 109

V
Vase 19, 22, 23, 28, 29, 35, 54, 57, 65, 78, 84, 86-88, 94, 125-127, 132, 138-140, 145-147, 152, 153, 156-158, 161, 163-165, 169, 172, 174, 187, 188
Vaseline 8, 29, 175
Victorian 137, 141, 147, 188
Visible Cooking Ware 8, 175

W
Wampum 149
Warwick 84, 125, 138, 147
Waverly 48, 49, 185
Wellington 68, 107, 177
Whirlpool 48, 167,
Wide Optic 126, 139, 152
Wide Panels 157
Wide Flat Panel 71
Windsor 40
Window Box 76, 101, 170
Winged Scroll 29, 63, 65-67, 98, 99
Winston 131
World 44
Wreath   189

Y
Yeoman 27, 30, 68, 79-81, 93, 94, 102, 119, 120, 129, 133, 134, 182, 183

Z
Zircon 18, 157-170